CONTENTS

TENNIS ANATOMY

E. Paul Roetert
Mark S. Kovacs

Human Kinetics

Library of Congress Cataloging-in-Publication Data

Roetert, Paul
  Tennis anatomy / E. Paul Roetert, Mark S. Kovacs.
    p. cm.
  ISBN-13: 978-0-7360-8936-4 (soft cover)
  ISBN-10: 0-7360-8936-5 (soft cover)
  1. Tennis--Training. I. Kovacs, Mark. II. Title.
  GV1002.9.T7R64 2011
  796.342--dc22

                                    2011006519

  ISBN-10: 0-7360-8936-5 (print)
  ISBN-13: 978-0-7360-8936-4 (print)

This publication is written and published to provide accurate and authoritative information relevant to the subject matter presented. It is published and sold with the understanding that the author and publisher are not engaged in rendering legal, medical, or other professional services by reason of their authorship or publication of this work. If medical or other expert assistance is required, the services of a competent professional person should be sought.

Acquisitions Editor: Laurel Plotzke-Garcia; **Developmental Editor:** Cynthia McEntire; **Assistant Editors:** Laura Podeschi, Claire Gilbert; **Copyeditor:** Patricia MacDonald; **Graphic Designer:** Fred Starbird; **Graphic Artist:** Kim McFarland; **Cover Designer:** Keith Blomberg; **Photographer (for illustration references):** Neil Bernstein; **Visual Production Assistant:** Joyce Brumfield; **Art Manager:** Kelly Hendren; **Illustrator (cover and interior):** Jennifer Gibas; **Printer:** United Graphics

Human Kinetics books are available at special discounts for bulk purchase. Special editions or book excerpts can also be created to specification. For details, contact the Special Sales Manager at Human Kinetics.

Printed in the United States of America   10   9   8   7   6   5   4   3   2   1

The paper in this book is certified under a sustainable forestry program.

Human Kinetics
Web site: www.HumanKinetics.com

United States: Human Kinetics
P.O. Box 5076
Champaign, IL 61825-5076
800-747-4457
e-mail: humank@hkusa.com

Canada: Human Kinetics
475 Devonshire Road Unit 100
Windsor, ON N8Y 2L5
800-465-7301 (in Canada only)
e-mail: info@hkcanada.com

Europe: Human Kinetics
107 Bradford Road
Stanningley
Leeds LS28 6AT, United Kingdom
+44 (0) 113 255 5665
e-mail: hk@hkeurope.com

Australia: Human Kinetics
57A Price Avenue
Lower Mitcham, South Australia 5062
08 8372 0999
e-mail: info@hkaustralia.com

New Zealand: Human Kinetics
P.O. Box 80
Torrens Park, South Australia 5062
0800 222 062
e-mail: info@hknewzealand.com

E4826

PREFACE

This book is written for serious competitive and recreational tennis players. Many tennis books emphasize fitness or strength and conditioning. *Tennis Anatomy* takes the next step and focuses on why and how you should get fit to play tennis. In this book, we highlight the different muscle groups involved in each of the strokes and show you how to best train those specific muscle groups as part of a comprehensive approach to tennis-specific training.

With the support of the United States Tennis Association (USTA), we provide the most up-to-date, relevant information on tennis conditioning available. As the national governing body of tennis in the United States, the USTA has a responsibility to grow and develop the sport. Through its player development program, the USTA shares the latest training techniques with competitive players in the United States. That mission encouraged us to take on this project and provide you with these training methods based on the anatomy of tennis.

Tennis was once considered a sport that could be played by people from age 8 to 80, but that range has expanded because of new training methods. The USTA offers 10 and Under Tennis for players age 10 and younger, who learn the sport while using modified equipment. In addition, national-level tournaments are offered for players age 90 and over. This shows the tremendous health, fitness, coordination, and psychological benefits that can be derived from the sport. Clearly, being a well-conditioned tennis player can assist in a long tennis career.

Of course the number of years someone can play is only one aspect of enjoying the game. The quality of play also is greatly enhanced by good training and conditioning. That is the true focus of this book. Whether you are getting in shape for league play, trying out for a high school or college team, or wanting to perform at a higher level in tournaments, this book provides you with up-to-date, practical training information based on the latest research available.

The first chapter provides an in-depth overview of the demands of the sport, the relationship of court surfaces and playing styles, the anatomy of each of the tennis strokes, and the physiological considerations of designing a training program. Chapters 2 through 7 systematically explain the role of each major body part in tennis play, focusing on muscle anatomy and its relationship to the strokes and providing specific exercises. Each exercise includes a tennis focus section that highlights how the exercise directly translates to improved on-court stroke performance or movement. Chapters 8 through 10 follow a similar format but highlight the importance of body rotation, movement skills, and injury prevention, respectively. The anatomical illustrations that accompany the exercises are color coded to indicate the primary and secondary muscles featured in each exercise and movement.

 Primary muscles   Secondary muscles   Connective tissues

You will enjoy and benefit from this information. Challenge yourself to learn more about the anatomy of your body as well as the tennis strokes, and improve your game by adding tennis-specific conditioning methods to your training. By incorporating these training techniques, you will surely be able to take your game to the next level.

ACKNOWLEDGMENTS

This book would not have been possible without the dedication, coaching, and support we have received over the years from the many sport science and medicine experts that have crossed our paths. All of our thoughts and ideas have been shaped by these dedicated people through courses, individual meetings, publications, and conferences. We cannot begin to name all of them, but we are truly indebted to them.

Another group of people instrumental in our lives is the many coaches and tennis teaching professionals who have taught us and helped us in the areas of player training as well as coaching education.

Human Kinetics came up with the idea and pursued our interest, and the United States Tennis Association (USTA) allowed us to take on this project. We very much appreciate the opportunity both organizations provided us. The Boca West Country Club made their tennis courts and fitness facilities available to us, for which we are very grateful.

Finally, we would like to thank our families, particularly Paul's wife, Barbara, and Mark's wife, Mary Jo, for their support and encouragement.

THE TENNIS PLAYER IN MOTION

Elite tennis players make it look so easy and effortless. By comparison, your movement skills, strokes, and fitness may leave something to be desired. Good coaches can help you improve technique and fitness, but keep in mind that there are many individual differences, even at the professional level. You can see that Roger Federer and Rafael Nadal don't play exactly the same way. They do have in common a desire to perfect their skills and a drive to continue to improve both technique and physical preparation. Proper technique, however, can be attained only if you can produce all necessary movements throughout the range of motion required for optimal positioning and stroke execution.

The sport of tennis requires strength, flexibility, power, endurance, and speed. Each of these components requires a well-trained muscular system. In addition, each court surface provides a different challenge. For example, clay courts require players to play longer rallies—sometimes as much as 20 percent longer—than do hard courts, and grass courts are even faster than most hard courts. Therefore, players who usually play on clay should train muscular endurance, while players who usually play on faster surfaces such as hard or grass courts may want to train more for muscular power or at least a combination of endurance and power.

Tennis is a lifelong sport, and the goal for many of us is to continue to enhance our performance while staying injury free, whether playing recreation-ally, in tournaments, at the college level, or even at the professional level. The best way to do this is to train effectively and use proper technique, seeking to produce effective and efficient tennis strokes. Consider the demands of tennis, but keep in mind your unique playing style and body structure.

Physical Demands of Tennis

Proper movement skills are critical for successful tennis. A successful tennis player must be able to get to the ball early and set up properly. Typically, this requires quite a few adjustment steps as you recognize the path, spin, and pace of the incoming ball. In fact, tennis often has been characterized as a game of emergencies. It involves constant movement, short sprints, and frequent directional changes. On average, 3 to 5 directional changes are required per point, and it is not uncommon for players to perform more than 500 directional changes during a single match or practice. Matches can last several hours, which requires aerobic fitness, but the short sprints, explosive movements, and directional changes are clearly anaerobic. Therefore, both the cardiore-spiratory and muscular systems should be trained using movement patterns representative of those seen during tennis play.

A big focus of the United States Tennis Association (USTA) Player Development training program is good movement and positioning. It is clear that if you can't get to the ball and set up properly, you won't hit the ball in the most balanced way to produce a forceful stroke. The legs are the first link in transferring forces from the lower to the upper body. This is part of the kinetic link, or kinetic chain, system. Newton's third law states that for every action there is an equal and opposite reaction. When you hit a tennis ball, your feet push against the ground, and the ground pushes back. This allows you to transfer force from one body part to the next, through the legs, hips, trunk, and arm all the way to the racket. The key is to do this in the most efficient and effective manner by timing the segments correctly, not leaving out any segments, and preparing your body to be strong and flexible enough to handle the stresses imposed. Proper technique and preparation of the muscular system should go hand in hand. The lower body, midsection (the core or torso), and upper body are important in tennis, but each segment has different needs and training requirements.

Training the legs is vital for efficient movement on the court. Research shows that the muscles in both legs are stressed equally in tennis, so training programs should reflect this. Since the vast majority of tennis movements are side to side, it is important to focus 60 to 80 percent of training on these movement patterns. In other words, working on lateral movements incorporating the abductors, the muscles that move the leg away from the center of the body, and the adductors, the muscles that bring the leg toward the center of the body, is at least as important as training the other muscle groups of the legs.

Think of the midsection of the body as a cylinder when it comes to training. Exercises should be designed to move the front, back, and side of the torso through multiple planes of motion. Tennis strokes require rotational movements as well as flexion and extension, frequently all in one stroke.

The dominant side of the upper body is much more involved in each stroke than the nondominant side. Therefore, in addition to training the dominant side for performance purposes, you need to train the nondominant side for balance and injury prevention. Since the game tends to be dominated by serves and forehands that involve the muscles of the front of the shoulders and the chest, be sure to train the muscles in the rear of the shoulders and the back. During forehands and serves, these muscles experience eccentric, or lengthening, contractions and shorten during the backhand stroke through concentric contractions.

When designing a training program for tennis players, it is important to balance upper and lower body, left and right sides, and front and back. *Tennis Anatomy* takes you through each of the body parts and provides you with appropriate exercises for optimal performance.

Playing Styles and Court Surfaces

Muscular balance is key for all players regardless of surface or playing style. However, your playing style and the surface you play on most often will influence your training goals and affect your exercise choices. For example, if you play a lot of long points on clay courts, you will want to train for endurance, especially in the lower body, instead of muscular strength and power, which would be more appropriate for a player who plays shorter points on hard courts. The same principle holds for the upper body, but to a lesser extent. You will still likely hit the ball just as hard when playing on a slower court; however, muscular endurance becomes more important since the points are longer. Regardless of playing style or surface, the upper body should be trained for both muscular power and endurance.

Playing Styles

Do you know what your playing style is? Do you like to come to the net and put the ball away with a volley or overhead? Or are you the type of player who likes to outlast your opponent by never missing a ball? Or do you like to hit the ball hard from the baseline, trying to dictate points and go for winners? All three styles can be very effective. Which style you use depends on your skills, personality, and possibly the court surface you play on most frequently. Most coaches categorize players into four different playing styles:

1. Serve and volleyer
2. Aggressive baseliner
3. Counterpuncher
4. All-court player

At the top professional level, the aggressive baseliner is the most prevalent, followed by the all-court player. The traditional serve and volleyer and the stereotypical counterpuncher are no longer preferred playing styles on either the men's or women's tours. However, tennis players at other levels can be seen playing each of these different styles.

The serve and volleyer (figure 1.1, page 4) relies on the serve to help dictate the point. After the serve, she explodes forward to the net. Typically, a serve and volleyer moves forward 20 to 40 percent more than a counterpuncher or an aggressive baseliner and about 20 percent more than an all-court player. Because of this forward movement, a serve and volleyer often finds herself at the net, trying to finish the point. Good volley technique is imperative and requires excellent leg strength, particularly in the quadriceps, gluteus maximus, and gastrocnemius. Strong leg muscles are key, especially for hitting low volleys that require significant knee flexion. Functional flexibility is very important to the serve and volleyer because she is required to get very low to the ground dozens of times throughout the match. Similarly, flexibility of the wrist is helpful, especially in reaching for volleys that stress the end range of the joint. This flexibility needs to be trained regularly.

The aggressive baseliner (figure 1.2, page 4) is more comfortable hitting groundstrokes but is also looking to put pressure on his opponent by hitting hard, aggressive strokes. This player's goal is to move less than the counterpuncher, and he prefers to move inside the court and take balls earlier to reduce the opponent's time between strokes. Muscular strength and

Figure 1.1   Serve and volleyer on a grass court hitting a low volley.

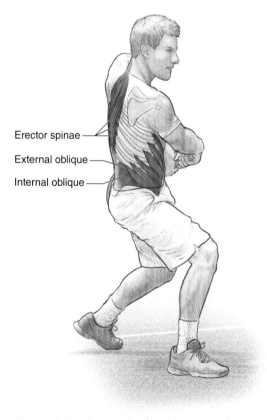

Figure 1.2   Aggressive baseliner on a hard court hitting a two-handed backhand.

endurance are required, but overall power is the major physical component that helps the aggressive baseliner dictate points. Having a major weapon such as a big forehand or strong two-handed backhand is very beneficial. Powerful strokes require strength as well as speed. Training exercises should take this into account. Exercises for the lower body and midsection should be very similar to those mentioned for players with other styles, but a greater emphasis on upper body power is helpful. The muscles of the chest and front of the shoulders are important for producing force, but don't neglect the muscles of the back of the shoulders and upper back. They help protect the shoulder complex and prevent injury.

The goal of the counterpuncher (figure 1.3) is to chase down every ball and make sure the opponent has to hit many balls each rally to win any points. This game style is based on great side-to-side movement and stroke consistency.

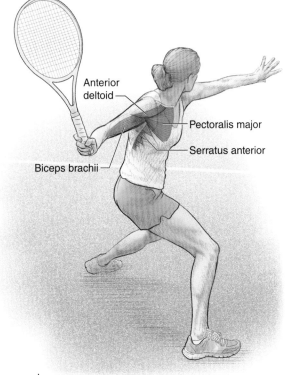

Figure 1.3 Counterpuncher on a clay court sliding to hit a wide forehand.

The counterpuncher moves laterally 60 to 80 percent of the time. Often she will stretch out to hit open-stance forehands or backhands. Therefore, it is critical to train the abductors and adductors as well as the muscle groups mentioned for the serve and volleyer in a well-rounded training program. This includes training flexibility as well as strength. The counterpuncher must depend on speed, quickness, and the ability to change direction since she may not often put the ball away for a winner. This type of game style is most effective on slower courts. Muscular endurance of the upper and lower body is critical. The obliques must be trained to assist in the rotational movements of all groundstrokes since the counterpuncher hits so many strokes, most with an open stance. Also, when playing great defense, the counterpuncher may hit many strokes when on one leg, out of position, or off balance. Therefore, it is imperative to train for these situations on the court by performing single-leg activities and training in unstable or irregular environments.

The all-court player (figure 1.4, page 6) looks to be aggressive when hitting groundstrokes but is also happy to follow aggressive shots to the net to finish points. All shots, from serves to groundstrokes to volleys, require equal attention in training. In addition, significant time should be spent on the transition game, training for shots that help the all-court player get to the net. The all-court player should regularly practice approach shots, such as a big forehand or slice backhand hit from half court, and follow each shot to the net. These shots require excellent movement and positioning, most often with a more closed stance than regular groundstrokes. Exercises for both the upper

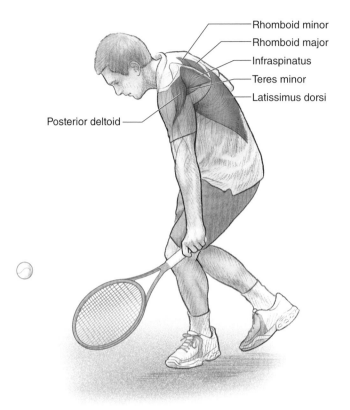

Rhomboid minor
Rhomboid major
Infraspinatus
Teres minor
Latissimus dorsi

Posterior deltoid

Figure 1.4   All-court player on a hard court hitting a one-handed slice backhand approach shot.

and lower body are beneficial, especially exercises that help develop weight transfer and movement into the court such as the spider drill (page 174) and the split step with stimulus drill (page 177) in chapter 9. It is important to train all muscle groups. The main focus should be on balancing between left and right, front and back, and upper and lower body.

Court Surfaces

Court surface does dictate playing style to a certain extent. In general, a serve and volleyer can be more successful on a faster grass court than on a clay court. A counterpuncher typically is more successful on a slower clay court than on any other surface.

Since balls bounce lower on grass courts and fast hard courts, players must be able to bend their knees well. Training should focus on exercises that take the body through the same range of motion expected during a match (e.g., full-range lunges and squats), with powerful recoveries. Players who play on clay often have to slide into their shots while hitting a wide forehand or backhand. Since playing on clay requires not only front and back leg strength but also muscular strength of the inside and outside of the legs, it is vital to train the abductors and adductors. Muscular endurance should be the focus. Researchers have compared the ball speed on hard courts and clay courts. After the ball lands on a clay court, the ball speed is typically reduced by 15 percent compared with the same ball on a hard court. This is a major reason why points are longer on clay courts and more strokes are hit per rally. Longer points on clay courts will slightly increase heart rate compared with shorter points on hard courts. Therefore, training to prepare for playing on a clay court will require a greater emphasis on aerobic conditioning versus training to play on a hard court. Service games are more physically demanding than return games, so players with weaker serves need to be prepared to play longer points and use a more physically demanding style.

Tennis Strokes

Tennis Anatomy features many exercises to improve your tennis game. Some are multijoint exercises, such as the lunge, which uses the hips, knees, and ankles. Others are single-joint exercises, such as the calf raise, which uses just the ankle joint. All exercises will be useful to prevent injuries and enhance performance. It is just as important to get fit to play tennis as it is to use tennis to get fit. Therefore, the exercises in the following chapters will help you prepare to take your game to the next level.

To identify how each exercise benefits your game, we provide icons to indicate the specific strokes—groundstrokes (forehand and backhand), serves and overhead shots, and volleys (forehand and backhand)—that will benefit from the conditioning exercise. In this section, we explain the major strokes and how actions, muscles, and muscle contractions are interrelated to produce effective and powerful strokes.

Forehand and Backhand Groundstrokes

Over the past 30 years, the greatest changes in tennis likely have occurred because of changes in racket technology. Rackets are made out of a variety of materials and are wider and stiffer, featuring a larger sweet spot. This has had a tremendous impact on the game, nowhere more than in the groundstrokes. The larger sweet spot is more forgiving on off-center hits, and the racket materials allow for more forceful swings. Because of these changes, forehand and backhand swings have changed as well. The long, flowing swings and follow-throughs in the direction of the target have given way to more violent, rotational swings that end up across the body in a variety of positions depending on the type of shot. These swing patterns allow players to hit the ball from a more open stance, particularly when hitting forehands but also when hitting two-handed backhands. This rotational component can put a significant amount of stress on the midsection. Therefore, exercises preparing the body for these stresses are vitally important.

Many of the muscle actions in the lower body are similar for all of the tennis strokes. There is an interplay between eccentric (lengthening) and concentric (shortening) actions that allows the body to store and release energy based on the phase of each stroke. In addition, each stroke requires trunk rotation, more so for groundstrokes, serves, and overheads than for volleys. The forehand, serve, and overhead strokes differ from one- and two-handed backhand strokes in that the upper body muscles are activated in the opposite way. The muscles in the upper back and back of the shoulder act concentrically (shorten) in the loading phase and eccentrically (lengthen) in the follow-through. The muscles of the chest and front of the shoulder first contract eccentrically during the backswing and then concentrically during the forward swing. The backhand swing follows an opposite pattern.

Forehand Groundstroke

The forehand groundstroke may be hit from an open stance, a square stance, or a closed stance. Each body position requires different lower and upper body mechanics, although all three stances use a combination of angular and linear momentum to power the stroke. Linear momentum is a product of both mass and velocity and can be generated in both a vertical and horizontal direction. Angular momentum refers to the rotational component of the stroke and takes into account both the moment of inertia about an axis (resistance to rotation about that axis) and the angular velocity about that axis. Both linear and angular momentum are fundamental for the successful generation of power in the forehand. The amount of linear momentum created affects the amount of rotational force that is generated about each of the body segments.

The open-stance forehand (figure 1.5) results in the greatest total body rotation and requires greater strength and flexibility throughout the core and lower body than the square-stance or closed-stance forehand. The square- and closed-stance forehands require less rotation at the core, and ball contact is made more in front of the player and closer to the net. It is important to understand that each of the stances is situation specific. In other words, where

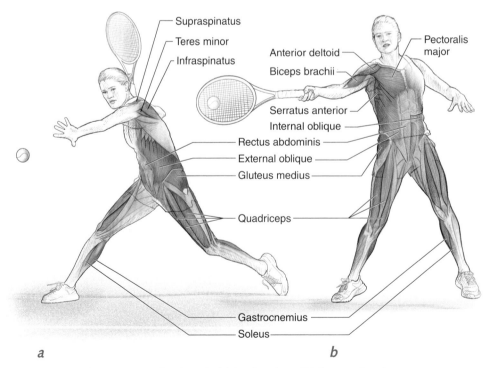

Figure 1.5   Open-stance forehand: *(a)* backswing; *(b)* forward swing.

you are on the court, the type of ball coming at you (both speed and spin), and the shot you are trying to hit often affect your stance.

The open-stance forehand is the most commonly used forehand in today's game. This shot requires vigorous hip and upper trunk rotation to provide effective energy transfer from the lower body through the core and into the racket and ball at impact. Trunk rotation, horizontal shoulder abduction, and internal rotation are the main motions that create racket speed in the forehand. After ball impact, eccentric strength helps decelerate the racket. This is particularly important as it relates to injury prevention.

During the backswing of the forehand groundstroke (figure 1.5a), the gastrocnemius, soleus, quadriceps, gluteals, and hip rotators contract eccentrically to load the lower legs and begin the hip rotation. The concentric contractions of the trunk rotation phase involve the ipsilateral internal oblique and contralateral external oblique, while the eccentric contractions pull in the contralateral internal oblique, ipsilateral external oblique, abdominals, and erector spinae. The concentric contractions of the shoulder and upper arm rotation in the transverse plane are performed by the middle and posterior deltoid, latissimus dorsi, infraspinatus, and teres minor and are followed by contractions of the wrist extensors. The eccentric contractions of the shoulder and upper arm rotation in the transverse plane are performed by the anterior deltoid, pectoralis major, and subscapularis.

During the forward swing (figure 1.5b), the gastrocnemius, soleus, quadriceps, gluteals, and hip rotators contract both concentrically and eccentrically to drive the lower body and hip rotation. Concentric and eccentric contractions of the obliques, back extensors, and erector spinae cause the trunk to rotate. The latissimus dorsi, anterior deltoid, subscapularis, biceps, and pectoralis major all contract concentrically during the acceleration phase to bring the racket to the ball for contact.

During the follow-through, the upper arm movement decelerates through the eccentric contractions of the infraspinatus, teres minor, posterior deltoid, rhomboids, serratus anterior, trapezius, triceps, and wrist extensors.

One-Handed Backhand Groundstroke

The one-handed backhand (figure 1.6, page 10) involves the summation of forces similar to the forehand, but there are important differences as well. The strength and muscular endurance of the wrist extensors are important for successful repeated performance of the backhand. Research has shown that torque at the wrist can create a rapid stretch of the wrist extensors, especially in players who have a history of tennis elbow (lateral epicondylitis).

For a one-handed backhand, the dominant shoulder is in front of the body. Typically, the stroke uses less trunk rotation; however, it requires a more coordinated action of the different body segments, including shoulder and forearm rotation, than the two-handed backhand. The front leg is more involved during a one-handed backhand than during a two-handed backhand. Similar racket speeds can be achieved with one- and two-handed backhands. Strength and flexibility, particularly of the muscles of the upper

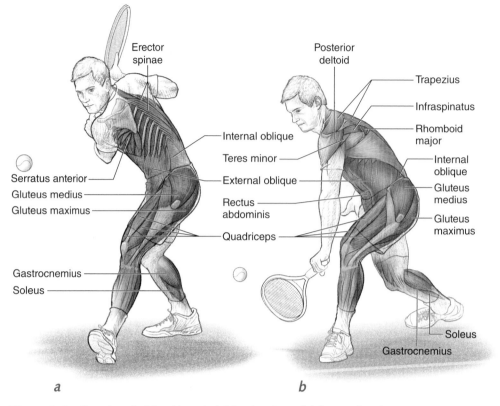

Figure 1.6 One-handed backhand: *(a)* backswing; *(b)* forward swing.

back and back of the shoulders, are key. Perform training exercises bilaterally to achieve muscular balance.

During the backswing of the one-handed backhand (figure 1.6*a*), the gastrocnemius, soleus, quadriceps, gluteals, and hip rotators contract eccentrically to load the legs and begin the hip rotation. The concentric contractions of the ipsilateral internal oblique and the contralateral external oblique are balanced by the eccentric contractions of the contralateral internal oblique, ipsilateral external oblique, abdominals, and erector spinae to rotate the trunk. The anterior deltoid, pectoralis major, subscapularis, and wrist extensors contract concentrically to rotate the shoulder and upper arm through the transverse plane as the posterior deltoid, infraspinatus, teres minor, trapezius, rhomboids, and serratus anterior contract eccentrically.

During the forward swing (figure 1.6*b*), the lower body and hip rotation is driven by the concentric and eccentric contractions of the gastrocnemius, soleus, quadriceps, gluteals, and hip rotators. Concentric and eccentric contractions of the obliques, back extensors, and erector spinae cause the trunk to rotate into the shot. The acceleration phase of the upper arm is performed through concentric contractions of the infraspinatus, teres minor, posterior deltoid, and trapezius.

During the follow-through, the subscapularis, pectoralis major, biceps, and wrist flexors contract eccentrically to decelerate the upper arm.

Two-Handed Backhand Groundstroke

Many players benefit from the two-handed backhand (figure 1.7), especially in the early learning stages. Both arms are used, increasing the power of the stroke, and fewer body segments are involved, which helps learning players coordinate the movement. These benefits help players hit balls in the strike zone and balls that bounce higher that must be hit above shoulder level. Although the two-handed backhand uses many of the same muscle groups as the one-handed backhand, the two-handed backhand requires greater trunk rotation versus the one-handed backhand. Therefore, the muscles of the torso and midsection should be well trained, especially the internal and external obliques. This is especially important in open-stance backhands, which are becoming more prevalent at all levels of the game. In addition, the legs should be trained to provide a stable base of support, to properly transfer the forces from the ground to the racket, and to provide endurance for long matches. One area unique to the two-handed backhand is the use of the nondominant arm and wrist. The flexors and extensors of the nondominant forearm and wrist and the muscles involved in ulnar and radial deviation must be trained appropriately.

During the backswing (figure 1.7a), the eccentric contractions of the gastrocnemius, soleus, quadriceps, gluteals, and hip rotators load the legs and begin the hip rotation. Concentric contractions of the ipsilateral internal oblique and contralateral external oblique are aided by eccentric contractions

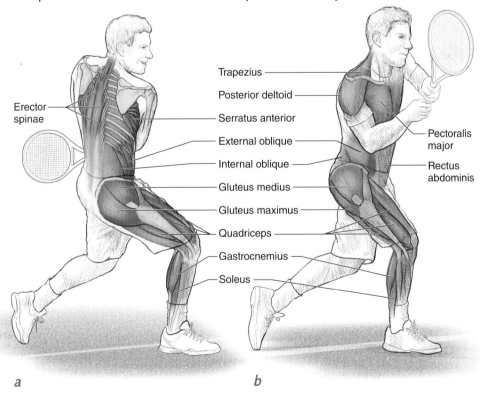

Trapezius
Posterior deltoid
Erector spinae
Serratus anterior
External oblique
Pectoralis major
Internal oblique
Rectus abdominis
Gluteus medius
Gluteus maximus
Quadriceps
Gastrocnemius
Soleus

a   *b*

Figure 1.7   Two-handed backhand: *(a)* backswing; *(b)* forward swing.

of the contralateral internal oblique, ipsilateral external oblique, abdominals, and erector spinae. The shoulder and upper arm on the dominant side rotate through the transverse plane through concentric contractions of the anterior deltoid, pectoralis major, subscapularis, and wrist extensors and eccentric contractions of the posterior deltoid, infraspinatus, teres minor, trapezius, rhomboids, and serratus anterior. On the nondominant side, concentric contractions of the middle and posterior deltoid, latissimus dorsi, infraspinatus, teres minor, and wrist extensors create the rotation of the shoulder and upper arm, assisted by eccentric contractions of the anterior deltoid, pectoralis major, and subscapularis.

During the forward swing (figure 1.7*b*), concentric and eccentric contractions of the gastrocnemius, soleus, quadriceps, gluteals, and hip rotators drive the lower body and hip rotation. Concentric and eccentric contractions of the obliques, back extensors, and erector spinae rotate the trunk. The upper arm on the dominant side moves to the ball through concentric contractions of the infraspinatus, teres minor, posterior deltoid, and trapezius. On the nondominant side, concentric contractions of the anterior deltoid, subscapularis, biceps, serratus anterior, and pectoralis major bring the arm to the ball.

During the follow-through, the dominant arm decelerates through eccentric contractions of the subscapularis, pectoralis major, and wrist flexors. The nondominant arm decelerates through eccentric contractions of the infraspinatus, teres minor, posterior deltoid, rhomboids, serratus anterior, trapezius, triceps, and wrist extensors.

Serves and Overheads

The serve is one of the most important shots in tennis. Each player starts half the points with a serve, for which he has time to prepare. The serve has become a true weapon in the game because it can dictate much of what happens in the ensuing point. Since the swing pattern of the overhead is quite similar to that of the serve, we are including it in this section as well.

From a strategy and tactics perspective, the main keys to a successful serve are pace, spin, and placement. The best servers combine all three components. Of course, physical preparation to develop strength, power, flexibility, and coordination determines the quality of these three components.

A good serve has become more important in professional tennis. Statistics from the 2009 U.S. Open Tennis Championships show that for the men's event, 5 of the top 10 ranked players also had the highest service speed. The women's game has followed a similar trend. You also can make the serve a true weapon by preparing your body for the rigors of serving at a high level for an entire match.

In the modern game, we see two types of serves: the foot-up serve (figure 1.8) and the foot-back serve (figure 1.9, page 14). Either serve is acceptable. Typically, the player chooses which serve to use based on personal preference and style. In the foot-up serve, the rear foot typically starts in the same position as for the foot-back serve. However, during the toss and backswing, the back foot slides up to join the front foot. This allows for more forward weight

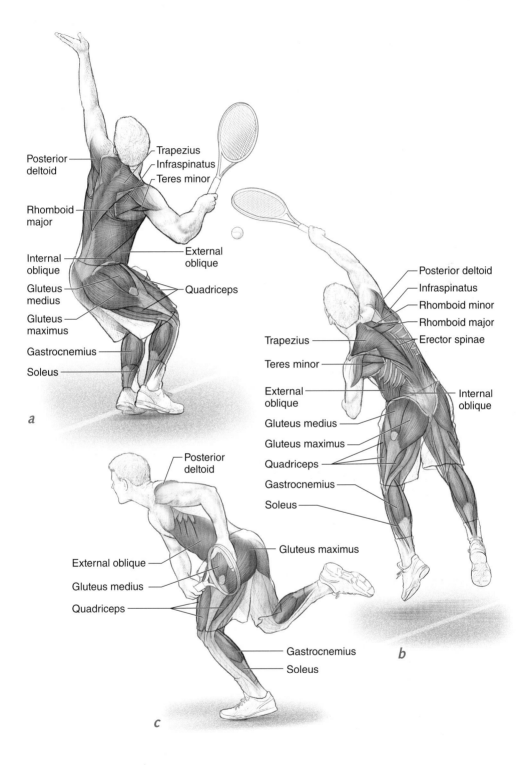

Figure 1.8 Foot-up serve: *(a)* loading; *(b)* acceleration; *(c)* follow-through.

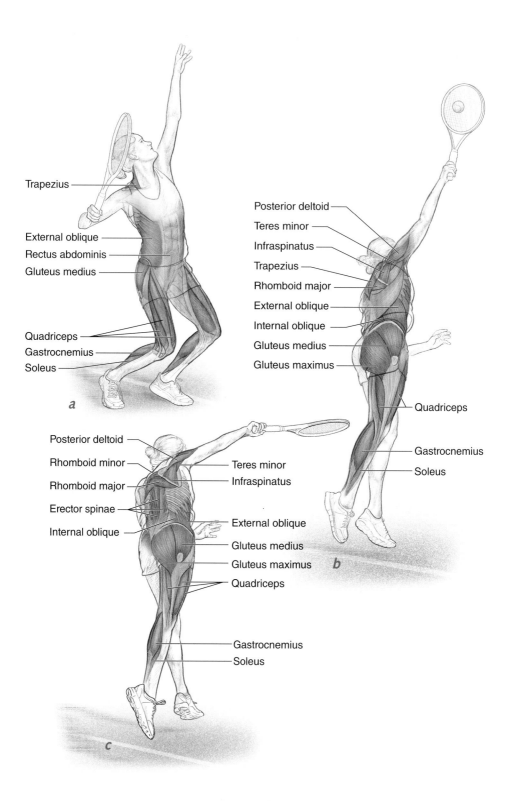

Trapezius

External oblique
Rectus abdominis
Gluteus medius

Quadriceps
Gastrocnemius
Soleus

a

Posterior deltoid
Teres minor
Infraspinatus
Trapezius
Rhomboid major
External oblique
Internal oblique
Gluteus medius
Gluteus maximus

Quadriceps

Gastrocnemius
Soleus

b

Posterior deltoid
Rhomboid minor
Rhomboid major
Erector spinae
Internal oblique

Teres minor
Infraspinatus

External oblique
Gluteus medius
Gluteus maximus
Quadriceps

Gastrocnemius
Soleus

c

Figure 1.9 Foot-back serve: *(a)* loading; *(b)* acceleration; *(c)* follow-through.

transfer as well as the ability to open up the hips easier during the forward swing. The foot-back position allows for a slightly more balanced position and possibly more upward (vertical) force production.

The execution of the serve or overhead has three major phases: loading, acceleration, and follow-through. During the loading (or preparation) phase, you are storing energy. The acceleration phase is when you release the energy through the end of ball contact. The last phase, the follow-through (or deceleration) phase, requires great eccentric strength to help control the deceleration of the upper and lower body.

A successful serve or overhead is the result of the summation of forces from the ground up through the entire kinetic chain and to the ball at impact. Knee flexion (eccentric contractions of the quadriceps) occurs to instigate effective ground reaction forces, the first major force-producing aspect of the service motion. This knee flexion often is defined as lower body loading. The gastrocnemius, soleus, quadriceps, gluteals, and hip rotators contract eccentrically to load the legs and begin hip rotation. During this stage of the serve or overhead, a counterrotation of the trunk, core, and upper body occurs to store potential energy that will ultimately be used in the service motion to transfer energy through impact. During this loading phase, a lateral flexion of the shoulders also increases potential energy storage. This energy will be released just before and during ball impact. The obliques, abdominals, and trunk extensors contract concentrically and eccentrically to rotate the trunk.

During the arm-cocking stage of the serve or overhead at the point of maximal external shoulder rotation, the dominant shoulder might be rotated as much as 170 degrees. The back extensors, obliques, and abdominals contract concentrically and eccentrically to extend and rotate the trunk. Concentric contractions of the infraspinatus, teres minor, supraspinatus, biceps, serratus anterior, and wrist extensors and eccentric contractions of the subscapularis and pectoralis major move the arm.

From this position there is an explosive vertical component that results in concentric contractions of the major muscles of the dominant arm and shoulder. The muscles in the front of the chest and trunk (the pectorals, abdominals, quadriceps, and biceps) are the primary accelerators of the upper arm, while the muscles in the back of the body (the rotator cuff muscles, trapezius, rhomboids, and back extensors) are the major decelerators during the follow-through. The leg drive is executed through concentric contractions of the gastrocnemius, soleus, quadriceps, and gluteals and eccentric contractions of the hamstrings. Concentric contractions of the abdominals and obliques and eccentric contractions of the back extensors flex and rotate the trunk. The elevation and forward movement of the upper arm are achieved through concentric contractions of the subscapularis, pectoralis major, anterior deltoid, and triceps. The elbow extends through the concentric contraction of the triceps and the eccentric contraction of the biceps. Concentric contractions of the latissimus dorsi, subscapularis, pectoralis major, and forearm pronators internally rotate the shoulder and pronate the forearm. Wrist flexion is created through the concentric contractions of the wrist flexors.

As a player lands, eccentric contractions of the gastrocnemius, soleus, quadriceps, and gluteals decelerate the body. Eccentric and concentric contractions of the back extensors, obliques, and abdominals flex and rotate the trunk. Eccentric contractions of the infraspinatus, teres minor, serratus anterior, trapezius, rhomboids, wrist extensors, and forearm supinators decelerate the upper arm.

The overhead motion and technique are similar to the service motion. This is particularly true when players keeps the feet on the ground when executing the overhead (figure 1.10). Typically, this overhead is used to return a short lob or when the ball bounces first. The muscular involvement is the same as for the serve; however, the swing pattern, especially the backswing, might shorten just slightly because of time constraints. The overhead with a scissor kick (figure 1.11) has a similar swing pattern for the upper body, but the lower body action includes a takeoff from the rear leg and a landing on the opposite leg after the ball is struck. This scissor-kick action produces force and helps with reach and balance during and after the shot. Significant concentric involvement from the gluteals, quadriceps, gastrocnemius, and soleus is required, particularly in the takeoff leg. These same muscles act as a shock absorber (eccentric contraction) in the landing leg.

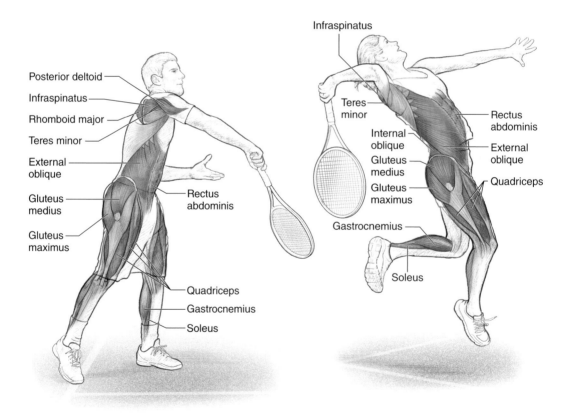

Figure 1.10   Follow-through after hitting an overhead with the feet on the ground.

Figure 1.11   Backswing before hitting a scissor-kick overhead.

Volleys

Although elite players don't come to the net as much as they used to since passing shots have improved significantly with new equipment, volleys are still an important part of the game, especially if you predominantly play doubles. The net game is still critical for doubles play at every level. Many points in doubles are won by a well-angled volley or put-away overhead. In addition, as players adjust to strong passing shots, they will learn new skills and methods related to attacking the net. All-court players in particular are continually looking for ways to end the point by moving forward. Many athletes who do not play at the professional level also look for a variety of ways to put away the ball.

Being fit enough to endure a long match while pressuring your opponent could be the difference between winning and losing. Coaches know that good volleys are hit with the feet as well as the hands. You have to be in proper position to volley well. Therefore, training the legs is probably the most important activity you can participate in to become a good volleyer. Lunges in all directions should receive particular attention because these movements mimic the on-court demands for volleying.

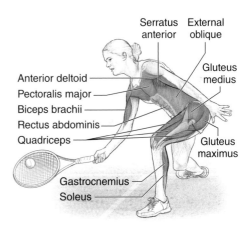

Figure 1.12　Closed-stance forehand volley at contact.

Since volleys require excellent movement skills, training the legs is key. Volleys require similar lower body movements as groundstrokes; however, the muscular actions may be more exaggerated. Greater flexion and extension at the hips, knees, and ankles in particular are likely. In addition, many of these movement patterns will be repeated at a faster speed the closer you are to your opponent. Muscles of the lower body need to be trained eccentrically as well as concentrically. Volleys are shorter strokes with an abbreviated backswing and follow-through compared with groundstrokes, although the same upper body muscles are used. Therefore, eccentric strength for the follow-through is key for immediate success and protection of the muscles surrounding the shoulder joint.

If players have time, they often hit volleys with closed stances (see figures 1.12 and 1.13). Since the swing is shorter, weight transfer becomes more important. Stepping forward facilitates the weight transfer.

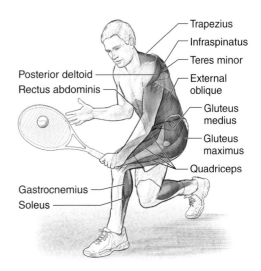

Figure 1.13　Closed-stance backhand volley at contact.

During the backswing of both the forehand and backhand volleys, the gastrocnemius, soleus, quadriceps, gluteals, and hip rotators contract eccentrically to load the lower legs and begin the hip rotation. The concentric contractions of the trunk rotation phase involve the ipsilateral internal oblique and contralateral external oblique, while the eccentric contractions pull in the contralateral internal oblique, ipsilateral external oblique, abdominals, and erector spinae. For the forehand volley, the concentric contractions of the shoulder and upper arm rotation in the transverse plane are performed by the middle and posterior deltoid, latissimus dorsi, infraspinatus, and teres minor and are followed by contractions of the wrist extensors. The eccentric contractions of the shoulder and upper arm rotation in the transverse plane are performed by the anterior deltoid, pectoralis major, and subscapularis. In the backhand volley, these concentric and eccentric actions are exactly opposite.

During the forward swing of both the forehand and backhand volleys, the gastrocnemius, soleus, quadriceps, gluteals, and hip rotators contract both concentrically and eccentrically to drive the lower body and hip rotation. Concentric and eccentric contractions of the obliques, back extensors, and erector spinae cause the trunk to rotate. For the forehand volley, the latissimus dorsi, anterior deltoid, subscapularis, biceps, and pectoralis major all contract concentrically during the acceleration phase to bring the racket to the ball for contact. For the backhand volley, the acceleration phase of the upper arm is performed through concentric contractions of the infraspinatus, teres minor, posterior deltoid, and trapezius.

During the follow-through phase of the forehand volley, the upper arm decelerates through the eccentric contractions of the infraspinatus, teres minor, posterior deltoid, rhomboids, serratus anterior, trapezius, triceps, and wrist extensors. During the backhand volley, the upper arm decelerates through the eccentric contractions of the subscapularis, pectoralis major, anterior deltoid, and biceps.

Training Considerations

Tennis Anatomy provides a number of exercises specific to tennis performance, targeting the muscles identified in this chapter. *Tennis Anatomy* also guides you beyond the exercises in this book to help you choose appropriate additional exercises to improve performance. A certified strength and conditioning specialist will be able to help you set up a training program specific to your needs and goals. This section covers some common training principles to help you get started on your way to becoming a well-conditioned player.

Adaptation

The body makes specific adaptations to training loads based on the load, intensity, type, volume, and frequency of training. Loads must be cyclical and progressive in order to produce continued improvement over time. Periodized programs are designed around cyclical progressive loading throughout the training year. A good periodized program can help you peak for important tournaments such as club or state championships or even the U.S. Open.

People will respond differently to the same training program. Age, gender, height, weight, training age, tennis goals, and motivation all influence how players respond to a specific training program. Some athletes respond well to training that is more frequent and higher in intensity; others may fail to respond to this kind of program. Monitor your individual response to the training program, and make sure to include recovery periods to permit higher intensity during key training sessions and competition.

Adaptations to most forms of training are easily reversible. If you do not continue to train at a high enough level, you will not maintain the improvements you have made, and your performance will regress. Detraining is the loss of the physiological benefits of training. In general, aerobic detraining is more rapid because it is based on decreases in aerobic enzyme concentrations. Muscle strength is more resistant to rapid detraining, but it will decline within a few weeks of reduced or limited training. Flexibility can increase and decrease rather rapidly as well.

Load and Intensity

To achieve training adaptations such as power, speed, strength, endurance, and flexibility, you must load the specific variable greater than you currently do. However, be careful to add an appropriate load. Too much load too soon can result in injury or overtraining, which can lead to long-term effects such as burnout.

In resistance training, loading is sometimes expressed as a percentage of the greatest load a person can lift during a specific movement, a one-repetition maximum, or 1RM. For example, this could be how much weight you could squat for one repetition. Training loads can be calculated as a percentage of this value. Depending on the goal of the training session, the load may be applied during one repetition of the movement or over a number of repetitions. If a 1RM lift is contraindicated for you or not desired, you can estimate your 1RM based on the number of repetitions you complete with a lighter resistance. It is nearly as accurate to base your 1RM on a 3RM or 5RM. Intensity is often measured and tracked via the percentage of resistance based on your 1RM. Use loads (intensities) that represent 60 to 100 percent of your 1RM. During a few periods throughout the year, loads may approach 100 percent intensity, but this occurs only for short periods of time as part of a structured, periodized training program.

Different intensities result in different adaptations. Athletes who spend the majority of their time training at between 60 and 80 percent of 1RM with larger overall training volumes exhibit greater hypertrophy gains (i.e., increase in lean muscle mass). To improve absolute strength, intensities need to be above 80 percent of 1RM, with more rest periods and lower overall total volume. To improve muscular endurance, train at an intensity below 60 percent of 1RM.

Volume

The volume of training typically is noted as the number of sets and number of repetitions performed in each set. The volume of the training stimulus is similar to the duration of an aerobic training program. Total workload is strongly related to many of the effects of a resistance training program. Although beginners may show improvement using a single set of a specific number of repetitions, continued improvement will require a total workload.

To see the greatest improvements, perform two or three sets of most exercises. The number of repetitions performed per set and the level of resistance used depend on the goals of that particular phase of training. A good rule of thumb is to perform two to four sets of 6 repetitions or less for strength, 8 to 15 repetitions for hypertrophy, and 15 to 30 repetitions for muscular endurance. Typically, tennis players should use no more than 20 repetitions per set and no less than 6 repetitions per set for proper strength gains and endurance improvement.

Frequency

Frequency is a component that needs to be adjusted for the individual tennis player. The beginner can improve with just two training sessions per week. Advanced athletes usually need more training sessions to adapt to the training load as desired. Train similar muscle groups two or three times per week. Include recovery time of at least 24 hours between training sessions that work the same major muscle groups.

Rest

Rest is often one of the most overlooked areas of a training program, yet it can provide the greatest improvement in performance and reduce the likelihood of injury. It takes approximately three minutes for your immediate energy stores to replenish after a short training bout (i.e., 10 to 60 seconds of activity). You need to understand this when creating a training program based on energy system development. For the nervous system, recovery is just as important and is usually harder to measure and monitor. Fatigue is obvious when you run for 90 seconds as fast as you can. This is metabolic (i.e., energy system) fatigue. If you performed a few depth jumps from an 18-inch (46 cm) box, you would not feel the same fatigue, but you would have fatigued different mechanisms, predominantly neural mechanisms. Recovery is required in both situations, but you might not allow enough recovery time for the second example because you may not feel tired.

Rest between exercises depends on the order of the exercise prescription. If the next exercise uses a different muscle group, the length of rest can be shorter. If the same muscle is trained in the next set, the length of rest between exercises should be similar to the time between exercise sets. If the training goal is to increase muscle hypertrophy, rest 30 to 90 seconds between sets. If absolute strength is the goal, increase rest time between sets to two or three minutes or even longer. If muscular endurance is the goal, keep rest periods brief (less than 30 seconds).

Variability and Progression

Variability includes variation in load, speed of movement, rest periods, and exercise selection. Without such variability, an athlete may experience training plateaus and perhaps undertraining or overtraining.

Variation in load should occur in a periodized manner based on the goals and objectives of your long-term development. For example, to increase maximal strength, your program should have a hypertrophy phase followed by a strength phase. To increase power, your program should progress from a hypertrophy phase to a strength phase to a power phase. For a more in-depth discussion of periodization, check out *Periodization: Theory and Methodology of Training* by Tudor Bompa and G. Gregory Haff (Human Kinetics, 2009).

Daily Program Organization

Aside from the overall periodization effect of a training program, there are particular methods of organizing a program at the daily workout level. Daily program design relies on your training age, goals, motivation, playing style, lifestyle, other responsibilities, and other factors; the type of training goals; and the time available for training. Several methods of daily program design are possible.

A full-body routine is often used with beginners, but it can be a good routine for advanced athletes or those with limited time for training. Divide the body into lower body, core, and upper body. Within these three broad areas, the body is further broken down. Exercises for the upper body include a press motion, press motion above the head, pull motion, and pull motion from above the head. Core exercises focus on flexion, extension, and rotation motion. Lower body exercises include squats and lunges as well as focus on ankle plantar flexion and dorsiflexion. Repeat the full-body program no more than four times a week, with at least one day's rest between sessions. In general, it takes three training days per week to make significant gains and two days per week to maintain strength.

A second option is the upper–lower two-on, one-off split routine. In this organization, the body is divided into two groups—upper and lower body. This program design is more appropriate for those who have some training experience. The upper body is trained on the first training day and the lower body on the second training day. Core training may be structured in parts or grouped into a separate training session. Consider, though, that the core is active in nearly every strength and conditioning exercise, and the core is trained in nearly all movements on and off the court. Follow each training day with one day off, and then begin the cycle again. This ensures adequate rest without the loss of potential training effects.

Tennis-specific training can be accomplished in many different ways. A systematic approach that involves a periodized plan and appropriate tennis-specific movements will provide the greatest results, improving on-court performance and reducing the risk of injury. Enjoy the exercises in *Tennis Anatomy* as they help you enhance your performance on the court and stay injury free.

For a tennis player, the shoulder may be the most important joint in the body. The shoulder is not only a major area of focus for performance enhancement but also one of the most commonly injured areas in tennis players. The shoulder joint, also called the glenohumeral joint, is a multiaxial ball-and-socket joint. This allows it to be the most mobile joint in the body, providing the largest range of motion. Having a large range of motion around the shoulder is a clear advantage for a tennis player because the sport requires movements in multiple directions, including stretching for wide groundstrokes, lunging for low volleys, and reaching up to hit deep overheads. This great range of motion in multiple planes, although beneficial, also creates a joint that is relatively unstable. As a result, shoulder injuries, typically from overuse, are common in tennis players. The exercises in this chapter both develop the shoulder muscles involved in tennis strokes and enhance the movements of the shoulder for improved performance.

Shoulder Anatomy

Three bones—the humerus, scapula, and clavicle—are primarily involved in the movements of the shoulder. The humerus, the long bone of the upper arm, articulates with the scapula, or shoulder blade, at the shoulder joint and with the radius and ulna, the bones in the forearm, at the elbow. The clavicle, or collarbone, is connected to the core of the body via the sternum. The clavicle forms part of the pectoral girdle and articulates with the scapula. As the shoulder joint moves, the muscles around the shoulder move the scapula to help increase the range of motion of the shoulder. Without scapular movement, the shoulder joint alone can move only to approximately 120 degrees of flexion or abduction. The movement of the scapula allows the shoulder joint to add approximately another 60 degrees of motion in each of these directions.

A number of muscles are involved in shoulder movement. The subscapularis, supraspinatus, infraspinatus, and teres minor muscles and their related tendons and ligaments make up the rotator cuff (figure 2.1, page 24), which is one of the most commonly injured sites of the shoulder, particularly as it relates to overuse injuries. (Shoulder injuries and other common tennis injuries are discussed in more detail in chapter 10, along with exercises for the prevention and rehabilitation of these injuries.) The muscles of the rotator cuff are relatively small muscles whose tendons cross the front, top, and rear of the head of the humerus. The rotator cuff plays a vital role in maintaining the humeral head in the correct position, supporting the more powerful muscle—the deltoid (figure 2.2, page 24)—of the shoulder region.

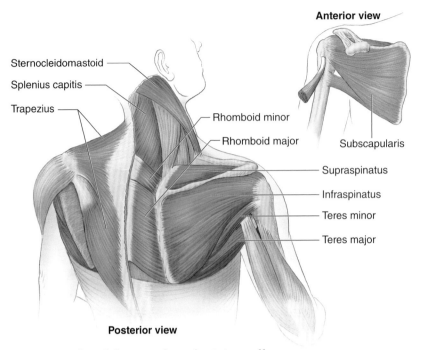

Sternocleidomastoid

Splenius capitis

Trapezius

Rhomboid minor

Rhomboid major

Anterior view

Subscapularis

Supraspinatus

Infraspinatus

Teres minor

Teres major

Posterior view

Figure 2.1   Muscles of the scapula and rotator cuff.

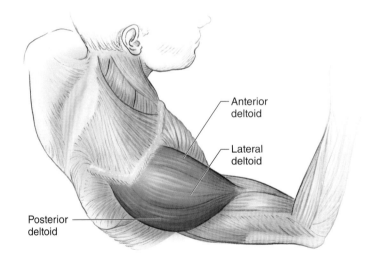

Anterior
deltoid

Lateral
deltoid

Posterior
deltoid

Figure 2.2   Deltoid muscle.

Technically, the shoulder complex consists of four joints—the sternoclavicular, acromioclavicular, glenohumeral, and scapulothoracic joints—that control the position of the humerus, scapula, and clavicle. The sternoclavicular joint connects the shoulder complex to the axial skeleton and allows for elevation and depression, protraction and retraction, and long-axis rotation of the clavicle. The acromioclavicular joint connects the clavicle to the acromion process of the scapula and contributes to total arm movement. The two principle movements are elevation and depression during abduction of the humerus and a gliding movement as the shoulder joint flexes and extends. The articular surfaces of the glenohumeral joint are the head of the humerus and the glenoid fossa of the scapula. The way both are curved allows for a great amount of motion in all directions yet also provides minimal stability. The scapulothoracic joint not only serves as a protective mechanism for someone falling with an outstretched arm but also assists with glenohumeral stability and enhances arm–trunk motion.

The deltoid, coracobrachialis, teres major, and rotator cuff group are the intrinsic muscles of the glenohumeral joint. These muscles originate on the scapula and clavicle and insert on the humerus. The latissimus dorsi and pectoralis major are the extrinsic muscles of the glenohumeral joint. These muscles originate on the trunk and insert on the humerus. The biceps brachii and triceps brachii also are involved in glenohumeral movement. Primarily, the biceps brachii assists in flexing and horizontally adducting the shoulder, and the long head of the triceps brachii assists in extension and horizontal abduction.

Muscular activity is greatest during the service motion. Therefore, the serve can be considered the most strenuous stroke in tennis. In the loading phase of the serve, which puts the shoulder in maximal external rotation, there is moderately high muscular activity of the supraspinatus, infraspinatus, subscapularis, biceps brachii, and serratus anterior, highlighting the importance of scapular stabilization exercises as well as anterior and posterior rotator cuff strength exercises. The acceleration phase, which begins with maximal external rotation and ends with contact, features high muscular activity of the pectoralis major, subscapularis, latissimus dorsi, and serratus anterior. These muscles are very active during the forceful concentric internal rotation of the humerus. During the follow-through phase after contact, the posterior rotator cuff muscles, serratus anterior, biceps brachii, deltoid, and latissimus dorsi show moderately high activity to help create eccentric muscle contractions to slow down the humerus and protect the glenohumeral joint.

Tennis Strokes and Shoulder Movement

For a tennis player, the shoulder is one of the most used (and sometimes overused) areas of the body. Typically, this makes it one of the most injured areas, especially in competitive tennis players. In addition to the repetitive demands on the shoulder, tennis also requires explosive movement patterns and highly intensive maximal-effort concentric and eccentric muscular work.

Groundstrokes require predominantly horizontal actions at the shoulder, using a combination of abduction and external rotation for the forehand backswing and backhand follow-through and a combination of abduction and internal rotation for the forehand forward swing and backhand backswing.

The tennis serve is a more complex sequence that uses a combination of horizontal and vertical movements. Horizontal abduction and external rotation occur during the backswing, with scapular retraction and depression into the loading phase. From the loading phase, scapular elevation, horizontal abduction, and shoulder extension move the arm toward contact. Internal rotation, shoulder extension, and adduction complete the follow-through. The muscles of the rotator cuff play a vital role in stabilizing the humerus in the shoulder during all tennis movements, but they are critical during the acceleration and follow-through phases of the serve (figure 2.3). The muscles of the rotator cuff aid in power production during acceleration and provide eccentric strength to help slow down the arm after contact during the follow-through. It has been reported that during the explosive internal rotation of the serve, shoulder rotation can reach speeds from 1,074 to 2,300 degrees per second. After contact, deceleration has to occur through eccentric strength of the rotator cuff and

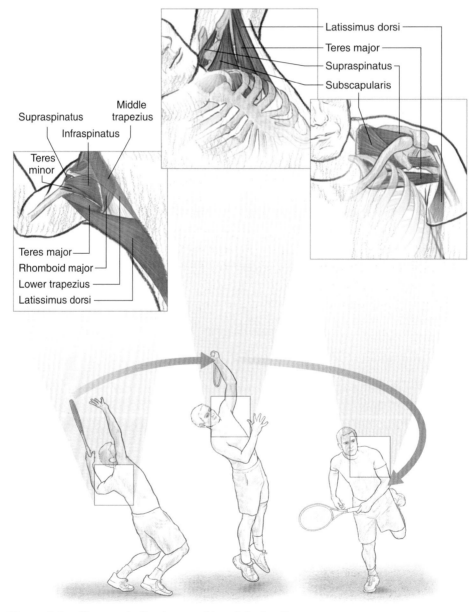

Figure 2.3   Changes in the humeral head during the serve.

related musculature. At the professional level, male players reach speeds on the serve close to 140 miles per hour (225 km/h). Proper preparation of the shoulder musculature is critical.

Tennis volleys require smaller muscle and joint movements than either groundstrokes or serves. For a forehand volley, slight external rotation and slight adduction followed by abduction of the shoulder allow the player to complete the stroke. The backhand volley involves slight internal rotation and abduction followed by slight external rotation and adduction of the shoulder.

Exercises for the Shoulder

The exercises that follow will benefit the shoulder joint. In particular, you will develop strong muscles surrounding the shoulder joint to both prevent injuries and enhance performance. While performing these exercises, contract the core muscles to develop a strong midsection. This will help with balance and posture as well as the transfer of forces from the lower to the upper body in each stroke. For exercises requiring resistance tubing, use a cable machine or attach the tubing to a stable object.

Although an exercise program should be highly individualistic, each exercise includes some general guidelines. An initial exercise program that includes the following exercises should include a proper balance between front and back and left and right sides of the body. We recommend starting with two or three sets of 10 to 12 repetitions until you have a strong base. Make sure you rest adequately between exercise sessions (at least one day) to help your muscles recover. Of course, the best training program is designed with your individual needs and performance goals in mind. Baseline fitness level, age, experience, and tournament schedule are all important factors. A certified strength and conditioning specialist with a good knowledge of tennis would be very helpful for designing a program as well as instructing on proper technique for each of the exercises.

Front Raise

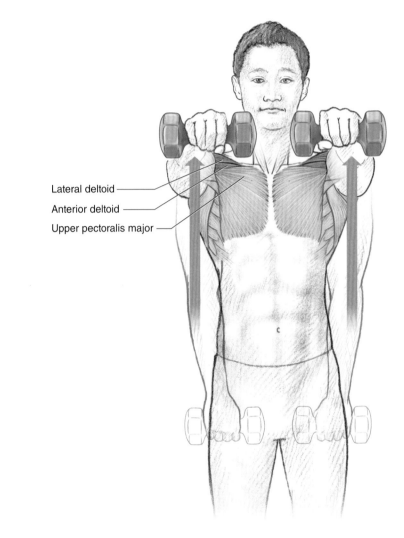

Lateral deltoid

Anterior deltoid

Upper pectoralis major

Execution

1. Stand straight with your shoulders back, squeezing your shoulder blades together. Hold a light dumbbell (less than 10 pounds [4.5 kg]) in each hand. Rest your hands in front of your thighs, palms turned down. This is the starting position.

2. While keeping the arms straight, elevate both arms to shoulder height, palms down. Lift the arms to the front of the body, out in front of the chest. Hold the weights at shoulder height for two seconds.

3. Slowly lower the arms to the starting position and repeat.

Muscles Involved

Primary: Anterior deltoid, lateral deltoid

Secondary: Upper pectoralis major

Tennis Focus

The anterior aspect of the shoulder is a major player in elevating the arm on forehand groundstrokes, especially on high balls. It is important to develop the anterior aspect of the shoulder because this directly influences the acceleration aspects of the groundstroke and serve. A weak anterior portion of the shoulder will require the muscles, tendons, and ligaments of the biceps and pectorals to perform more work than is necessary, and this could result in injury.

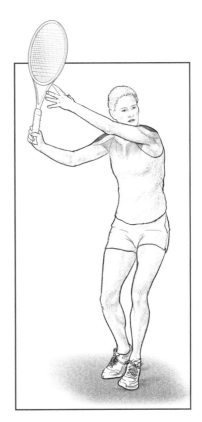

Lateral Raise

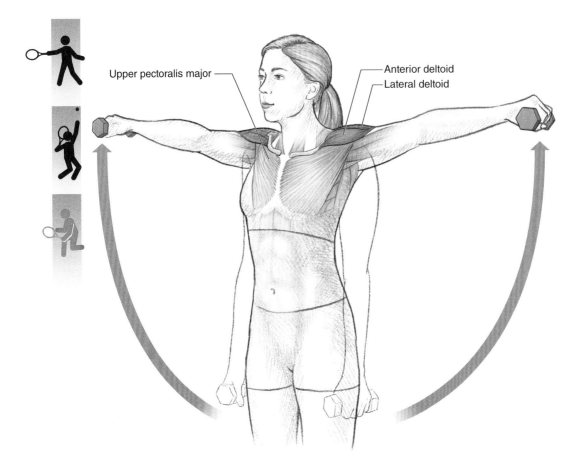

Upper pectoralis major

Anterior deltoid
Lateral deltoid

Execution

1. Stand straight with your shoulders back, squeezing the shoulder blades together. Hold a light dumbbell (less than 10 pounds [4.5 kg]) in each hand. Rest your hands on the outsides of your thighs, with palms facing your thighs.
2. While keeping the arms straight, elevate both arms out to the sides (abduction), bringing the weights to shoulder height while keeping the palms turned down. Maintain firm wrists and straight arms. Hold for two seconds.
3. Slowly lower the arms to the starting position and repeat.

Muscles Involved

Primary: Anterior deltoid, lateral deltoid

Secondary: Upper pectoralis major

Tennis Focus

The lateral aspect of the shoulder region, specifically the lateral portion of the deltoid muscle, is important in all movements requiring the arms to abduct away from the body. This is a component seen during tennis strokes, specifically in the backhand ground-stroke from the end of the backswing all the way through the follow-through. Although the rotator cuff muscles help stabilize the shoulder joint during tennis strokes, having a strong and fatigue-resistant deltoid muscle will help protect the shoulder even more. It is especially important for those who use a one-handed backhand stroke because the lateral deltoid is one of the major muscles involved in both the acceleration and deceleration aspects of the stroke. The lateral deltoid also is important during the backswing component of the serve as the arm is in abduction.

Bent-Over Rear Raise

Deltoid

Rhomboid minor

Rhomboid major

Teres major

Execution

1. Stand with the feet shoulder-width apart. With a slight bend in the knees, flex at the waist while keeping the back straight. Hold a light dumbbell (less than 10 pounds [4.5 kg]) in each hand. Extend the arms toward the ground, palms turned down. Bend the elbows to about 90 degrees, knuckles toward the floor.

2. While keeping an approximate angle of 90 degrees at the elbows, slowly raise the forearms, leading with the dumbbells, to shoulder height. Hold for two seconds.

3. Slowly lower the arms to the starting position and repeat.

Muscles Involved

Primary: Deltoid

Secondary: Teres major, rhomboid major, rhomboid minor

Tennis Focus

The posterior aspect of the shoulder is a major player in decelerating the arm after a tennis stroke. It is necessary in all strokes, but the greatest forces are seen in the deceleration of the arm after ball contact in the serve. It is important to have adequate strength in the muscles at the back of the shoulder. This will aid in the development of strength in a movement that directly correlates with the backhand groundstroke. Squeezing the shoulder blades together (retraction) at the top of the movement activates the rhomboids to a greater extent, which helps develop appropriate scapular control and prevent shoulder injuries.

Elbow-to-Hip Scapular Retraction

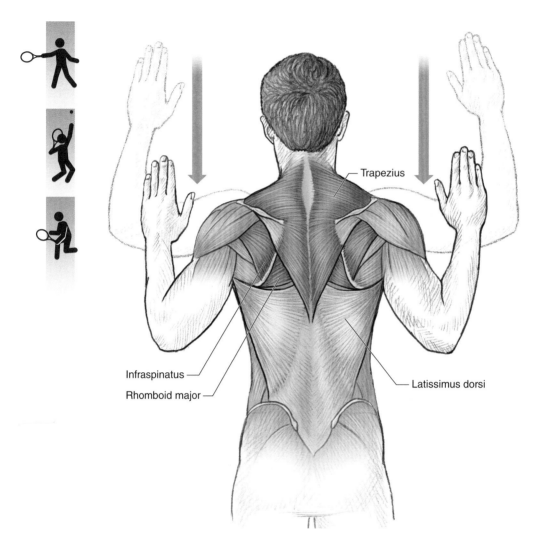

Trapezius

Infraspinatus

Rhomboid major

Latissimus dorsi

Execution

1. Stand erect with feet shoulder-width apart and knees slightly bent, with a 90-degree angle at the shoulders and a 90-degree angle at the elbows. This is the starting position.
2. Slowly lower the elbows toward the hips in a controlled manner by contracting the rhomboids in the upper back. Hold at the bottom of the movement for two to four seconds.
3. Slowly raise the arms to the starting position and repeat.

Muscles Involved

Primary: Trapezius, infraspinatus, rhomboid major, rhomboid minor

Secondary: Latissimus dorsi

Tennis Focus

Scapular position plays a role in an athlete's risk of injury. The elbow-to-hip scapular retraction exercise is focused on the muscles that are involved in maintaining good scapular position. This exercise is a posture-predominant movement and is particularly important because many tennis players have weaker than required scapula-stabilizing musculature. The focus of this exercise is to strengthen the muscles

involved in stabilizing the scapula, which will not only aid in the prevention of injury but also allow for more efficient stroke mechanics, resulting in greater power production on tennis strokes. Apart from improving posture, this exercise directly stimulates muscle contractions similar to those experienced during the loading phase of the serve and also during forehand volleys with a close contact position.

External Rotation

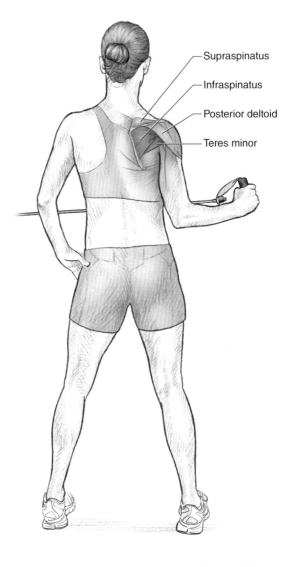

Supraspinatus

Infraspinatus

Posterior deltoid

Teres minor

Execution

1. Stand sideways and grab the resistance tubing with your outside hand, your elbow close to the hip at a 90-degree angle and your forearm parallel to the floor. This is the starting position.

2. Slowly rotate the shoulder externally (away from the body) against the resistance from the tubing, making sure the forearm remains parallel to the floor. Maintain your shoulder position, and do not rotate the waist during the movement. Hold near the end range of motion for two seconds.

3. Slowly return to the starting position, and repeat for 10 to 12 repetitions. Then perform the same movement with the opposite arm.

Muscles Involved

Primary: Infraspinatus, teres minor

Secondary: Supraspinatus, posterior deltoid

Tennis Focus

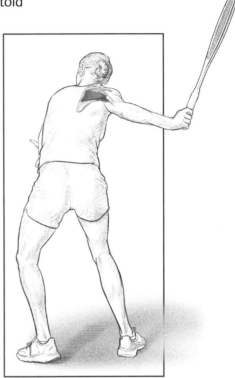

Rotator cuff strength and endurance are paramount for success in tennis, whether you want to hit serves at 130 miles per hour (210 km/h) or be able to endure a three-hour match without fatigue or pain. Train the rotator cuff muscles regularly to prevent injury and improve performance. The external rotation exercise focuses on the external rotators and is very important in decelerating the arm after ball contact. External rotation is a crucial factor in many tennis strokes, including the forehand backswing. During the backswing, the arm is abducted. A strong shoulder helps store potential energy to be released during the follow-through phase of the forehand. Because this exercise is performed in the transverse plane, it is highly specific to improving deceleration after ball contact on groundstrokes. Having the appropriate strength to effectively decelerate the arm is important for preventing shoulder and arm injuries.

VARIATION

Place a towel between the elbow and side during the external rotation exercise. This creates a better position for performing the exercise and also increases the muscle activation of the posterior aspect of the shoulder—the infraspinatus and teres minor—by approximately 20 percent.

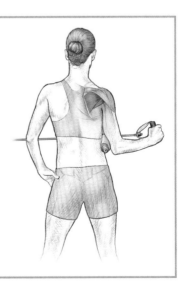

90/90 External Rotation With Abduction

Supraspinatus

Posterior deltoid

Teres minor

Infraspinatus

Execution

1. Stand erect, feet shoulder-width apart, facing the tubing attachment. Grasp the resistance tubing at shoulder height with a 90-degree angle at the shoulder and a 90-degree angle at the elbow. This is the starting position.

2. Slowly externally rotate the shoulder against the resistance. The forearm starts parallel to the floor and is perpendicular to the floor at the top of the movement (external rotation at the shoulder). Hold near the end range of motion for two seconds.

3. Slowly return to the starting position, and repeat for 10 to 12 repetitions. Then perform the same movement with the opposite arm.

Muscles Involved

Primary: Infraspinatus, teres minor

Secondary: Supraspinatus, posterior deltoid

Tennis Focus

Similar to the external rotation exercise, the 90/90 external rotation with abduction exercise focuses on the external rotators, which are very important in decelerating the arm after ball contact. Because this exercise is performed in the sagittal plane, it is highly specific to improving the ability to decelerate the arm after ball contact on serves. It also is important during the concentric contractions of the loading phase of the serve. This exercise requires good shoulder capsule stability and helps strengthen the muscles required to decelerate the arm after a serve.

90/90 Internal Rotation With Abduction

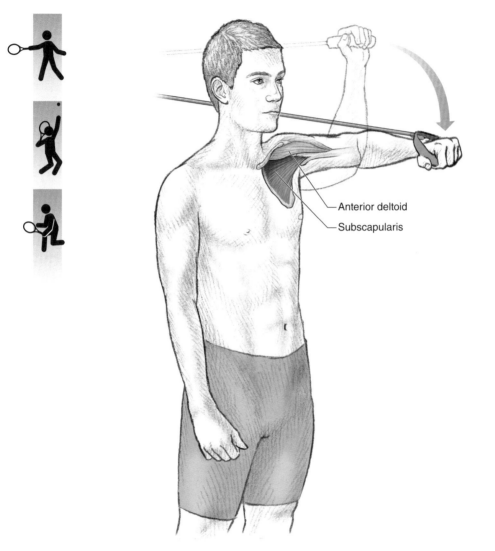

Anterior deltoid
Subscapularis

Execution

1. Stand erect with feet shoulder-width apart, facing away from the tubing attachment. Grab the resistance tubing at shoulder height, with a 90-degree angle at the shoulder and a 90-degree angle at the elbow. This is the starting position.

2. Slowly internally rotate the shoulder against the resistance. The forearm starts perpendicular to the floor and is parallel to the floor at the bottom of the movement. Hold near the end range of motion for two seconds.

3. Slowly return to the starting position, and repeat for 10 to 12 repetitions. Then perform the same movement with the opposite arm.

Muscles Involved

Primary: Subscapularis

Secondary: Anterior deltoid

Tennis Focus

A strong rotator cuff is important in tennis, especially just before and during ball contact. The 90/90 internal rotation with abduction exercise specifically focuses on strengthening the smaller stabilizing muscles required to maintain shoulder position. Because this exercise is performed in the sagittal plane, it is highly specific to improving the strength of the stabilizers during the acceleration phase of the serve. This exercise will increase the speed of the serve as the player's capability to produce power improves throughout the contact and follow-through phases of the serve.

Low Row

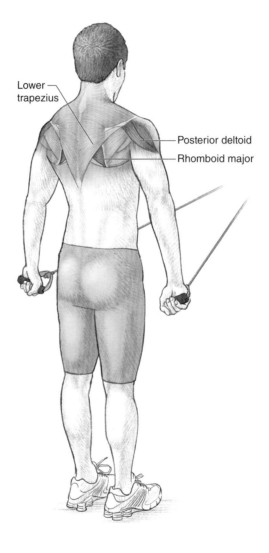

Lower trapezius

Posterior deltoid

Rhomboid major

Execution

1. Stand erect and face the tubing attachment. With your arms low and in front of you, grasp the resistance tubing in each hand. Activate the rhomboids by squeezing the shoulder blades together.

2. Slowly push your hands back against the resistance while keeping your arms straight. Maintain a stable wrist position. Hold near the end range of motion for two seconds.

3. Slowly return to the starting position and repeat.

Muscles Involved

Primary: Posterior deltoid, rhomboid major, rhomboid minor

Secondary: Lower trapezius

Tennis Focus

Tennis players must be well balanced in their muscular development. The low row exercise focuses on the muscles of the upper back and posterior shoulder that are typically undertrained in tennis players—the posterior deltoid, rhomboids, and even the lower aspects of the trapezius. The low row helps prevent injuries and strengthen the vital muscles used to help the upper body decelerate after a powerful groundstroke or serve. These muscles are also active concentrically in the acceleration phase of the one- and two-handed backhand. Another benefit of the low row exercise is improved scapular position and shoulder alignment at rest. Proper posture limits the likelihood of shoulder impingement–related pain, tightness, or weakness in the anterior aspect of the shoulder and chest muscles. Shoulder impingement, specifically at the front of the shoulder, results in pain and potentially reduced stroke speed. Long-term impingement can result in more severe injuries that may require surgery. It is important to improve shoulder posture to prevent these injuries.

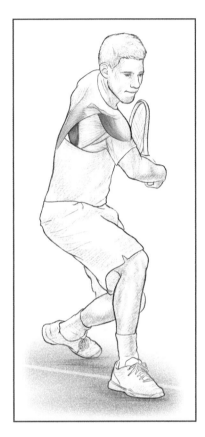

As a tennis player builds ground reaction forces from the ground up, these forces are transferred sequentially through the legs, hips, trunk, shoulder, arm, and racket to form a linked system. This kinetic link, or kinetic chain, provides the basis for a rhythmic motion and produces force as well. For a tennis player, the arm and wrist link the lower body and torso to the racket, which is the last link before ball contact. If the arms and wrists are not strong or flexible, the power produced throughout the lower body and core will not efficiently transition into the ball. This results in reduced power on the stroke and spin.

Arm and Wrist Anatomy

The elbow divides the arm into a lower and an upper component. The elbow is a hinge joint restricted to two movements—extension and flexion. Elbow extension occurs when you straighten your arm from a 90-degree angle at the elbow. Elbow flexion is the opposite; you decrease the angle at the elbow by bringing the forearm closer to the upper arm. The bone that links the elbow to the shoulder is the humerus. The lower arm, typically called the forearm, is supported by the radius and ulna.

The primary elbow flexors are the biceps brachii and the brachialis (figure 3.1). The biceps has two heads—one long and one short—both of which cross the shoulder joint and attach to the scapula. Besides being an elbow flexor, the biceps contributes to the forearm movement of supination, which is the position of the arm when the palm is turned up. Pronation describes the movement of the arm when the palm is turned down. The brachialis lies beneath the biceps and arises at the midpoint of the humerus. It attaches to the ulna just after it passes anteriorly to (in front of) the elbow joint. A smaller muscle that sometimes contributes to elbow flexion is the brachioradialis. This muscle arises

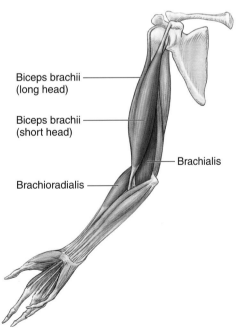

Biceps brachii (long head)

Biceps brachii (short head)

Brachialis

Brachioradialis

Figure 3.1 Biceps brachii, brachialis, and brachioradialis muscles.

from the lateral aspect of the humerus just above the elbow and travels along the outer part of the forearm to attach to the radius just above the wrist joint.

The primary elbow extensor is the triceps brachii (figure 3.2). *Triceps* refers to the three heads of proximal attachment of the muscle, and *brachii* refers to its origination in the arm. The medial and lateral heads of the triceps arise from attachment sites on the humerus, and the long head crosses the shoulder joint and arises from the scapula (shoulder blade). The three heads unite to form the tendon that crosses behind the elbow joint and inserts onto the olecranon process of the ulna. The olecranon process forms the tip of the elbow when it is bent to 90 degrees. A much smaller triangular muscle called the anconeus assists the triceps in extending the elbow joint and is important as an elbow stabilizer. The anconeus is intimate with the lateral head of the triceps; sometimes the fibers of the two muscles blend into one another.

The forearm muscles consist of flexors and extensors (figure 3.3). As the name suggests, the pronator teres pronates the forearm. In concert with the brachioradialis, palmaris longus, flexor carpi radialis, and flexor carpi ulnaris, the pronator teres also assists in flexing the forearm. The anconeus, extensor carpi radialis longus, extensor carpi radialis brevis, and extensor digitorum extend the forearm. The extensor carpi ulnaris extends the wrist. Each of these muscles is important in transferring forces to the racket and in stabilizing the elbow and wrist. In addition to flexion and extension, the wrist also abducts and adducts—important movements in the modern tennis game, particularly in relation to the swing path of the forehand and backhand. The extensor carpi radialis longus is the primary abductor of the wrist, while the extensor carpi ulnaris is the primary adductor of the wrist. These motions are

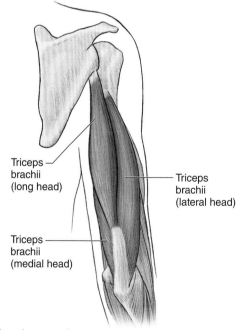

Triceps brachii (long head)

Triceps brachii (lateral head)

Triceps brachii (medial head)

Figure 3.2 Triceps brachii muscle.

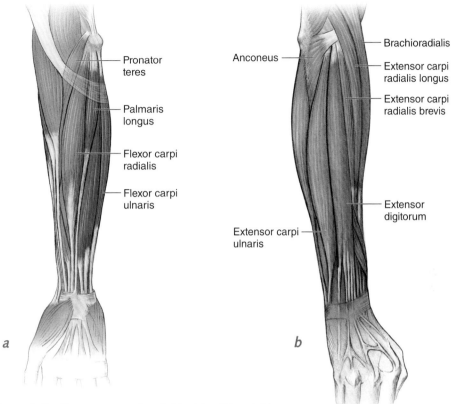

Figure 3.3 Forearm muscles: *(a)* inside; *(b)* outside.

also often referred to as ulnar flexion (adduction) and radial flexion (abduction), or sometimes as ulnar and radial deviation.

There is a real interplay between concentric and eccentric contractions throughout the tennis strokes, especially in the upper and lower arm muscles. For example, during the forward swing (acceleration) phase of the forehand stroke, concentric contractions of the anterior deltoid, subscapularis, and pectoralis major produce upper arm horizontal movement and internal rotation. The latissimus dorsi and wrist flexors act concentrically as well, while the forearm pronators, which pronate the forearm, and biceps, which extends and flexes the elbow, alternate concentric and eccentric contractions.

In the forward swing (acceleration) phase of the one-handed backhand, the infraspinatus, teres minor, posterior deltoid, and trapezius contract concentrically to produce upper arm abduction and horizontal extension. The triceps contracts concentrically to extend the elbow, and the wrist extensors and adductors contract concentrically to extend and adduct the wrist. The biceps contracts eccentrically to extend the elbow. In the two-handed backhand, these same muscles are active on the dominant side. However, some muscles also contract on the nondominant side during the acceleration phase. The anterior deltoid, subscapularis, biceps, serratus anterior, pectoralis major, and wrist flexors and abductors contract concentrically for upper arm adduction and horizontal flexion. Volleys follow a muscular pattern similar to the respective groundstrokes.

During the acceleration phase of the serve, the subscapularis, pectoralis major, anterior deltoid, and triceps contract concentrically to produce upper arm elevation and forward movement. The triceps contracts concentrically to extend the elbow. The latissimus dorsi, subscapularis, pectoralis major, and forearm pronators contract concentrically to produce shoulder internal rotation and forearm pronation. The wrist flexors contract concentrically to flex the wrist.

Tennis Strokes and Arm and Wrist Movement

Tennis has evolved much over the past 30 years, due in part to racket and string technology. Because of these advances, we see many more open-stance groundstrokes. The strokes have become more violent, requiring more strength to help protect the surrounding joints, especially for the arm muscles. The muscles of the upper arm must contract concentrically to provide force for the different strokes, but they also need to provide eccentric strength to slow down the swing during the follow-through. We have seen an increase in wrist injuries due to the more vigorous radial and ulnar deviations modern rackets allow. Strengthening the flexors and extensors and the abductors and adductors is a must. Proper balance in each of these muscle groups is the key.

The triceps at the back of the upper arm is an important muscle for a tennis player because it provides support for the shoulder and elbow. From a performance perspective, the triceps plays an important role in the serve, overhead, backhand, and volley. For example, one of the last segments of the kinetic chain in a tennis serve or overhead is extension at the elbow just before contact with the ball. This motion is produced by a forceful contraction of the triceps that transfers forces from the trunk and upper arm into the racket. From an injury prevention perspective, a strong triceps alleviates stress on the wrist, elbow, and shoulder joints, reducing the risk of injury. Because tennis is played with a racket and matches can last many hours, grip and forearm strength and muscular endurance are vital for a tennis player to develop. The more grip and forearm strength a tennis player has, the less stress she will place on the wrist and elbow joints. Sufficient forearm and grip strength also can reduce the likelihood of shoulder-related injuries. A player who has a weak grip or forearm may try to overcompensate with the shoulder, increasing the risk of injury.

Exercises for the Arms and Wrists

When applied correctly, the following exercises will develop arm strength and muscular balance. In general, you want to strengthen the dominant and nondominant arms equally. This is appropriate for both the upper and lower arms, even though the dominant arm will develop more strength because of the nature of the sport. Strengthening exercises should focus on muscular balance and endurance. Therefore, we recommend you use lighter weights and more repetitions, especially for the lower arms. Weights typically won't exceed 8 pounds (3.63 kg), and the number of repetitions will usually be 12 to 15 unless otherwise noted. Movements in several directions that are similar to the movement path of the strokes should be incorporated into a training program and have been outlined in the following exercises. Properly strengthened arms will help you perform better on the court and also protect the shoulders, elbows, and wrists from injury.

Triceps Cable Push-Down

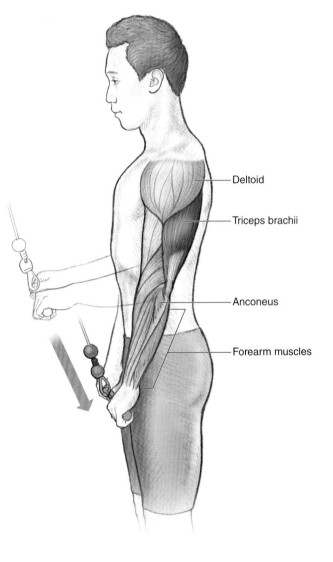

Deltoid

Triceps brachii

Anconeus

Forearm muscles

Execution

1. Stand with your feet together and your core contracted. Grasp the short bar of a cable or pulley machine in a shoulder-width overhand grip. Begin with the bar at waist level, elbows bent at approximately 90 degrees.

2. Keeping the upper back straight and upper arms stiff, push the bar down to the thighs. The only movement should be the extension at the elbow joint. You will feel the triceps contract during this movement. Hold in the down position for two seconds.

3. Slowly return to the starting position and repeat.

Muscles Involved

Primary: Triceps brachii

Secondary: Deltoid, anconeus, forearm muscles

Tennis Focus

During the backswing of the serve and overhead, the triceps muscle is put "on stretch" to store potential energy, which is transferred into usable kinetic energy during the forward swing of the serve or overhead. During the forward swing, the triceps contracts concentrically just before, during, and after ball contact, which helps transfer the energy produced throughout the lower body and core into the racket and ball. During both one- and two-handed backhand groundstrokes, a similar muscle contraction sequence occurs, the major difference being that the serve requires a more vertical swing path, whereas the backhand results in more of a horizontal swing path. Both the forehand and backhand volleys involve triceps contraction, but these contractions are predominantly isometric. The elbow joint does not lengthen or shorten

substantially during the stroke, but the triceps still contracts to ensure solid ball contact and appropriate power in the stroke. Triceps strength and muscular endurance are major preventive factors in reducing the likelihood of arm and shoulder injuries.

VARIATION

Triceps Rope Push-Down

Using a rope attachment for the triceps push-down causes a forcible pronation at the wrist, which targets the lateral (outer) head of the triceps. The lateral head of the triceps is important in the end ranges of the backhand stroke as well as the volley follow-through. The development of the lateral head can improve performance in these strokes while also reducing the likelihood of injury.

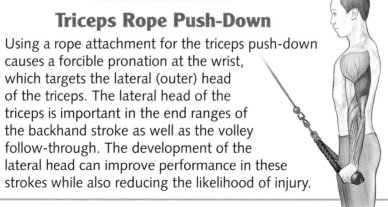

Half Dip

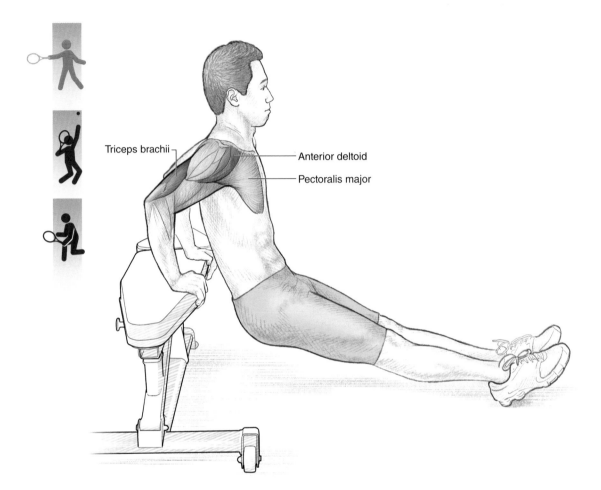

Triceps brachii

Anterior deltoid

Pectoralis major

Execution

1. Face away from a weight bench. Place your hands palms down on the edge of the bench, with your fingers pointing forward. Straighten your legs, with your heels on the floor and toes pointed up. (You can instead place your heels on another bench of the same height for greater resistance.) In the starting position, the arms are mostly straight, elbows bent between 150 and 180 degrees.

2. Slowly bend at the elbows, lowering the torso until the upper arms are close to parallel to the floor. Maintain an upright torso.

3. Push down into the bench, focusing on concentrically contracting the triceps to straighten your arms until the elbows return to the starting position. Repeat.

Muscles Involved

Primary: Triceps brachii, anterior deltoid

Secondary: Pectoralis major

Tennis Focus

The half dip, or modified dip, is preferred for tennis players over a full
dip. The half dip targets the triceps
more than the anterior deltoid and
pectoralis major, which are targeted
more in a full dip. Because of the high
risk of shoulder injuries in tennis, it is
important to limit anterior shoulder
discomfort and impingement. An athlete performing half dips is still able
to strengthen the triceps and reduce
the likelihood of shoulder injury. From
a performance perspective, developing strong triceps muscles in multiple
planes of motion helps develop greater
overall power in the tennis strokes.
In the loading phase of the serve, for
example, the strength and range of
motion of the triceps are crucial to
effectively transition from the storing
of energy to the release of energy into
the acceleration phase of the serve.

<hr>

VARIATION

Alternative Grips

If you have access to parallel bars, you can perform the half dip on the
parallel bars. The standard grip, palms facing together with thumbs
forward, hits all three heads of the triceps, while the major focus is on
the inner long head. Reversing the grip on the parallel bars to turn the
palms out with the thumbs backward switches most of the focus to
the long head of the triceps. However, this movement may be difficult
for people who do not have adequate wrist strength. The benefit is
that it works the muscle at a different angle, yet the technique is more
advanced.

Cable Overhead Triceps Extension

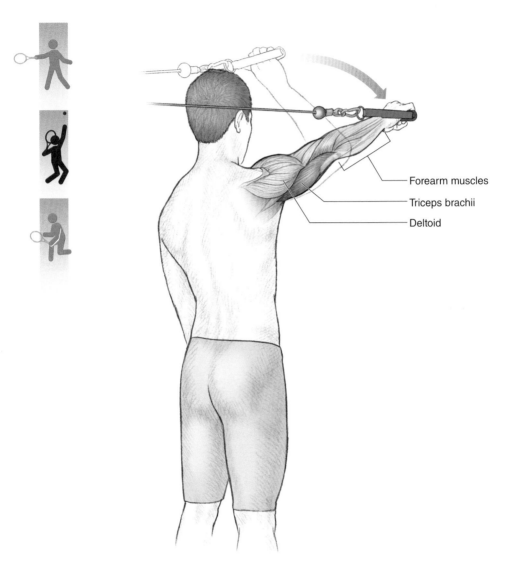

Forearm muscles

Triceps brachii

Deltoid

Execution

1. Stand upright, feet together, and face away from the cable or pulley machine. Grasp the handle in one hand. Start with your arm bent, with approximately a 90-degree angle at the elbow.

2. Slowly extend your arm forward by contracting the triceps until the elbow straightens. Maintain a stable core and shoulder position.

3. At the end of the movement, pause and then slowly return the handle to the starting position via an eccentric triceps contraction. Repeat the movement for 10 to 12 repetitions, and then switch to the opposite arm.

Muscles Involved

Primary: Triceps brachii

Secondary: Deltoid, forearm muscles

Tennis Focus

Similar to the previous two exercises, the cable overhead triceps extension strengthens the triceps for both injury prevention, particularly of the shoulder and elbow joints, and performance enhancement (more powerful serves, overheads, and backhands). The upward phase of the swing in the serve and overhead requires significant triceps extension just before contact as well as during and immediately after contact. The cable overhead triceps extension exercise is highly specific to the serve and overhead movement. It develops the triceps to contract in a similar plane of movement to that experienced during the serve and overhead.

Hammer Curl

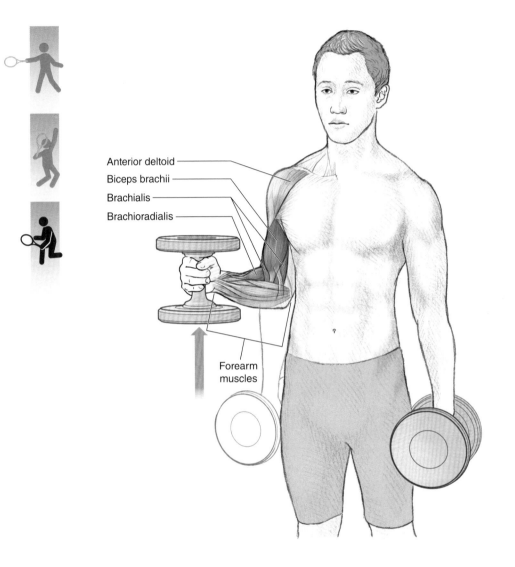

Anterior deltoid
Biceps brachii
Brachialis
Brachioradialis

Forearm muscles

Execution

1. Stand with a stable lower body position. Hold a dumbbell in each hand, arms extended by your sides with your core contracted.

2. Lift one dumbbell toward your shoulder in a straight path by bending the elbow to approximately 90 degrees while maintaining a stable core and lower body position. Pause at the end of the movement, and slowly lower the dumbbell to the starting position.

3. Repeat with the other arm. Alternate arms for 10 to 12 repetitions.

Muscles Involved

Primary: Brachialis, brachioradialis, biceps brachii

Secondary: Anterior deltoid, forearm muscles

Tennis Focus

Because tennis requires the player to handle a tennis racket for hours during a match, sufficient grip and forearm strength and muscular endurance are important. The forearm and wrist are the last major areas of energy transfer up through the kinetic chain—the summation of forces from the ground up—and on to the racket. Therefore, strength development through this region will aid in the transfer of power from the body to the racket and subsequently to the ball for greater speed and spin on each shot. The muscles developed in this exercise play a role in the follow-through of both forehand and backhand groundstrokes. On the forehand, the deceleration of the arm during the backswing is partially aided by the contractions of the biceps, brachialis, and brachio-

radialis, which support the more overworked decelerators of the shoulder. During the backswing and follow-through on the backhand groundstroke, especially the two-handed stroke, the biceps is recruited to help support the other muscles around the shoulder and upper back.

VARIATION

Hammer Curl With Rotation

In the standard hammer curl, the dumbbell moves in a straight path to the anterior deltoid. The hammer curl with rotation begins in the same position, but as the elbow starts to bend, the thumb rotates out (forearm supination), which activates the biceps to a greater extent. The biceps connects to the forearm muscles that are engaged during forehand volleys and any other time the racket face is open so the thumb points out.

Wrist Roller

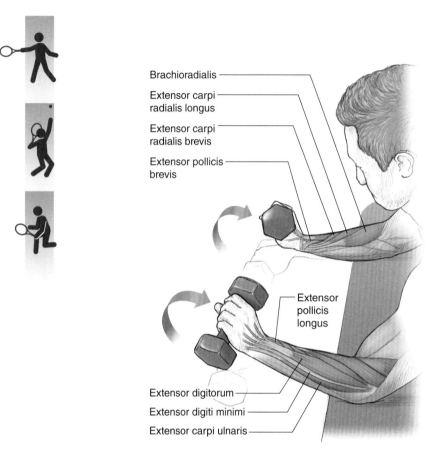

Brachioradialis

Extensor carpi radialis longus

Extensor carpi radialis brevis

Extensor pollicis brevis

Extensor pollicis longus

Extensor digitorum

Extensor digiti minimi

Extensor carpi ulnaris

Execution

1. Kneel beside a weight bench. Prop your elbows on the bench, with your arms bent at approximately 90 degrees. Grasp two dumbbells using an overhand grip (palms turned down). Place your forearms on the edge of the weight bench.

2. Lower the dumbbells by flexing your wrists. Attempt to point your knuckles toward the floor.

3. Raise the weight by contracting the forearm extensors so that the knuckles point toward the ceiling. Repeat for 10 to 12 repetitions.

Muscles Involved

Primary: Forearm extensors (brachioradialis, extensor carpi radialis longus, extensor carpi radialis brevis), extensor digitorum, extensor carpi ulnaris, extensor pollicis brevis, extensor pollicis longus

Secondary: Finger extensors and flexors

Tennis Focus

Muscular endurance of the forearm is critical for performance and injury prevention, particularly around the wrist and elbow joints. The wrist provides the final joint action before contact with the ball. At this point, all forces have been collected to create a forceful shot. Wrist flexion and extension exercises aid in the development of a firm wrist for each of the tennis strokes.

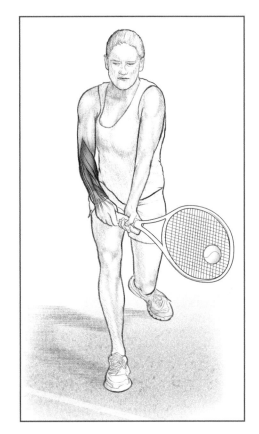

VARIATION

Barbell Wrist Roller

You also can perform this exercise with a barbell. Grasp the barbell in an overhand grip (palms down). Perform the exercise as described with the dumbbells.

Wrist Curl

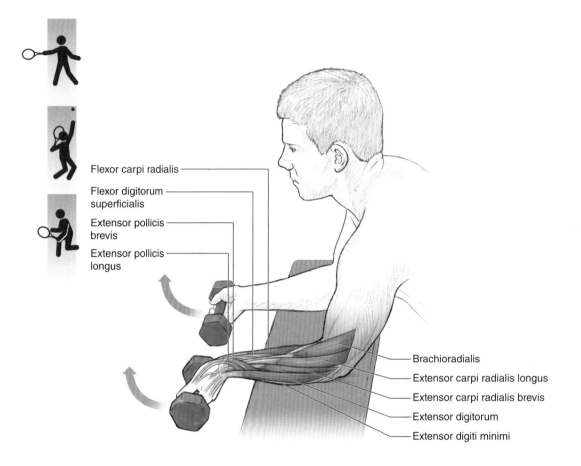

Flexor carpi radialis

Flexor digitorum
superficialis

Extensor pollicis
brevis

Extensor pollicis
longus

Brachioradialis

Extensor carpi radialis longus

Extensor carpi radialis brevis

Extensor digitorum

Extensor digiti minimi

Execution

1. Kneel beside a weight bench. Prop your elbows on the bench, with your arms bent at approximately 90 degrees. Grasp two separate dumbbells using an underhand grip (palms turned up). Place your forearms on the edge of the weight bench.

2. Lower the dumbbells by bending (extending) your wrists, pointing your knuckles toward the floor.

3. Raise the weight by contracting the forearm flexors. Repeat for 10 to 12 repetitions.

Muscles Involved

Primary: Forearm extensors (brachioradialis, extensor carpi radialis longus, extensor carpi radialis brevis), extensor digitorum, extensor carpi ulnaris, extensor pollicis brevis, extensor pollicis longus, flexor carpi radialis

Secondary: Finger extensors and flexors

Tennis Focus

Forearm strength is important from a number of perspectives. Forearm rotation (pronation and supination) and flexion and extension help prepare the muscles for repeated stresses from each of the strokes. In addition, open stances and modern equipment have changed the game. These advances, particularly new racket technology, allow for more forceful groundstrokes incorporating both ulnar and radial deviation. A well-rounded training program for the arms and wrists should incorporate each of these exercises.

V A R I A T I O N

Barbell Wrist Curl

You can also perform this exercise with a barbell. Grasp the barbell in both hands using an underhand grip (palms up). Perform the same movement as described with the dumbbells.

Forearm Supination

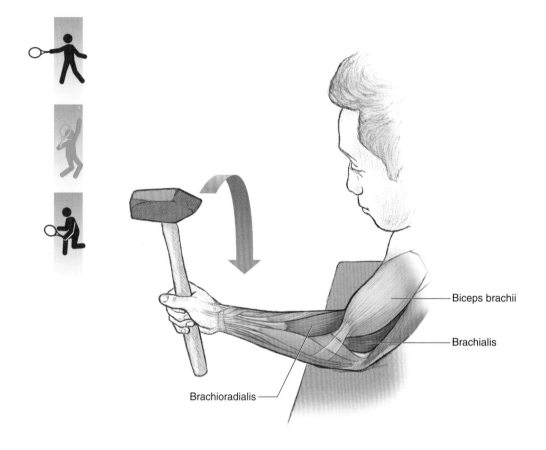

Biceps brachii

Brachialis

Brachioradialis

Execution

1. Sit or kneel beside a weight bench. Position your forearm and elbow on the bench. Establish a stable and rigid shoulder position. Grasp a hammer or other piece of equipment with a weighted head in one hand. Begin with the hammer head pointed to the ceiling.

2. Slowly and with control rotate your forearm. Take two to four seconds to rotate your forearm to avoid using momentum. If the hammer is in your right hand, your thumb will move to the right as you rotate your forearm. At the end of the movement, hold the position for two seconds, and then slowly return to the starting position.

3. After performing a set with one arm, switch arms and perform the same movement pattern on the other arm.

Muscles Involved

Primary: Brachioradialis, brachialis, supinator (anterior)

Secondary: Biceps brachii

Tennis Focus

During the backswing and follow-through of a two-handed tennis stroke, the top hand facilitates supination of the forearm. Developing appropriate strength and endurance in the forearm muscles will help with shot execution and also reduce the risk of wrist and shoulder injuries. Forearm supination helps involve the wrists in the stroke, allowing for greater spin and the potential to create angles that would not be possible without this movement. Developing strength in the forearm is also very beneficial to improve performance on both the forehand and backhand volley as well as the slice backhand.

Forearm Pronation

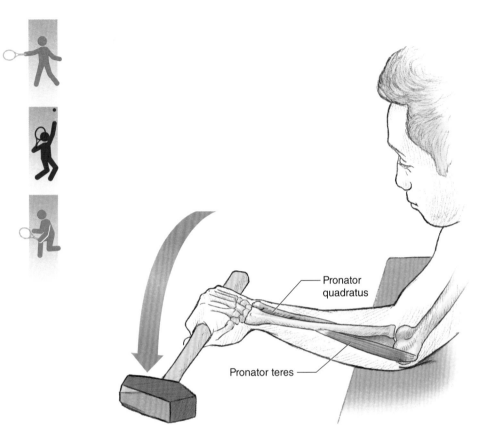

Pronator
quadratus

Pronator teres

Execution

1. Sit or kneel beside a weight bench. Place your forearm and elbow on the bench. Establish a stable and rigid shoulder position. Grasp a hammer or other piece of equipment with a weighted head in one hand. Begin with the hammer head pointed to the ceiling.

2. Slowly and with control rotate your forearm. Take two to four seconds to rotate the forearm to avoid using momentum. If the hammer is in your right hand, your thumb will move to the left as you rotate your forearm. At the end of the movement, hold the position for two seconds, and then slowly return to the starting position.

3. After performing a set with one arm, switch arms and perform the same movement pattern on the other arm.

Muscles Involved

Primary: Pronator teres, pronator quadratus (anterior)

Tennis Focus

Wrist and forearm pronation play leading roles in tennis strokes, especially during the forward swing of the tennis serve. Appropriate strength and endurance in the forearm pronators will provide added spin and speed to your serve while also helping to prevent wrist, elbow, and shoulder injuries. Forearm pronation is most evident in the tennis serve and overhead. It occurs just after the internal shoulder rotation of the dominant arm during the serve and overhead. Forearm pronation also is seen in baseball pitchers and football quarterbacks after they release the ball. In tennis, forearm pronation sometimes is referred to as wrist snap, but it involves a lot more of the upper body and arm than just the wrist.

In many sports and athletic activities, the chest muscles often are a main focus of training. In tennis the chest muscles serve several purposes. First, tennis requires balance. Proper muscular balance between the anterior (front) and posterior (back) of the body is critical for achieving good performances on the court and staying injury free. Second, training the chest muscles properly will help create the powerful movements required in tennis and also improve muscular endurance.

Characterizing muscles as either chest or back muscles is not always easy because several muscles—such as the pectoralis minor and serratus anterior—wrap around the body or are located deep below other muscles. For the purposes of this book, we will characterize the pectoralis minor and serratus anterior as chest muscles.

Chest Anatomy

The pectoral girdle, which connects the upper limbs to the skeleton, is made up of the scapulae and clavicles. The pectoral girdle muscles (figure 4.1, page 68) hold the scapulae and clavicles in place. The pectoralis major connects to the sternum, clavicle, and costal cartilages. Its main responsibility is to pull the arm toward the body (adduction). The pectoralis minor attaches to the coracoid process of the scapula and assists in pushing the arm forward (protraction). Similarly, the serratus anterior performs protraction. It wraps around the wall of the rib cage and attaches to the scapula's inner edge.

As mentioned in chapter 2, the deltoid covers the shoulder joint. A well-developed deltoid gives the shoulder a rounded appearance. The anterior deltoid is the front of the large deltoid muscle and, in concert with the pectoralis major and other muscles, is very active in the upper arm horizontal movements required by the forehand and serve. In this respect, the anterior deltoid assists the chest muscles in horizontal flexion, or adduction. The triceps brachii, discussed in chapter 3, is a powerful arm extensor that lies posterior to the humerus at the back of the arm. Although the triceps is not actually a chest muscle, it is heavily recruited to help the chest muscles in all pressing movements. Because it links the shoulder with the elbow, the long head of the triceps helps stabilize the shoulder joint in all pressing and overhead movements. For example, both forehand and backhand volleys combine an upper arm horizontal movement with elbow extension. The triceps works in conjunction with chest muscles such as the pectoralis major to produce a forward pressing motion. A similar action occurs during the forward or upward part of the swing.

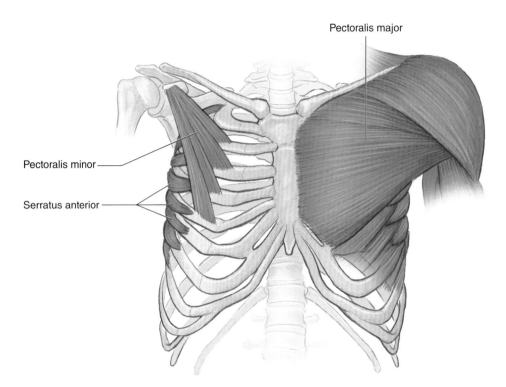

Figure 4.1   Muscles of the chest.

The triceps contracts to extend the elbow, while the chest muscles contract to provide forward movement of the upper arm and shoulder.

Tennis Strokes and Chest Movement

A strong chest helps during pushing actions and actions that pull the arms toward the body. The tennis strokes that benefit the most from these actions include the serve and overhead, forehand groundstroke, and forehand volley. The serve and overhead have more of a vertical component to their movement pattern than any other stroke. The chest muscles are stretched in the backswing (loading) phase and are contracted concentrically in the forward or upward swing toward contact and into the follow-through. A similar pattern of muscle activation is seen during the forehand groundstroke and volley, although the movement pattern is more horizontal. Strong chest muscles are key when hitting balls above shoulder level, especially high bouncing balls with topspin. Significant strength is needed to hit these balls outside the typical strike zone and with enough force and spin to gain control of that specific point. This concept also holds for balls that are hit from a stretched position while you are reaching for a particularly wide or low shot. The key is to train these muscles in concert with the back muscles and those muscles that facilitate body rotation. Both superficial and deep muscles require attention. Since tennis can produce some imbalances in the upper body, strength training programs should focus on a proper balance of the different muscle groups. Balance of right and left sides in the chest muscles is important, as is a balance between the muscles of the chest and back. This not only can affect performance but more important can prevent injuries as well.

Because all the muscles of the pectoral girdle are involved in every stroke as either prime movers (in the serve, overhead, forehand, and forehand volley) or as stabilizers (in the backhand and backhand volley), these muscles require careful attention. The main focus is muscular endurance, which will allow you to hit strong shots throughout long matches. Appropriate strength, power, and muscular endurance in the chest muscles also improve posture and balance. From a performance standpoint, good posture and balance facilitate direction changes, help you set up properly for each shot, and allow quick recovery between shots. The chest muscles, even when not serving as the primary muscles in a specific tennis stroke, often play an important secondary role. In addition to the benefits directly related to performance, strong chest muscles prevent injury and encourage proper posture. The upper body, which is part of the trunk, needs to act as a strong link between the lower body and the dominant arm to transfer the ground forces throughout the stroke. Further, a good balance between chest and upper back muscles will help you achieve proper posture, which may prolong your tennis career and increase the stroke velocity and power you provide to each stroke.

The chest muscles are most active in the forward swing of the serve, overhead, and forehand. It is estimated that at the top level, almost 75 percent of all tennis strokes are forehands and serves. Because of this, muscular endurance is as much a priority as muscular power. Most of the actions of the chest muscles, especially in the forward swing, are concentric in nature, meaning the muscles contract and shorten during the motion. To help prepare these muscles for this shortening action, training programs should reflect this same activity.

Exercises for the Chest

Proper muscular balance between chest and back muscles is important for both performance and injury prevention. Be sure to alternate front and back exercises. For example, you could perform these exercises on different days. The general guideline is two or three sets of 10 to 12 repetitions, especially while building a strong foundation. It is also important to address both dominant and nondominant sides to maintain balance between the two sides. To this end, most chest exercises are bilateral. Muscular endurance for withstanding long matches is as important as strength and power. Monitor the amount of weight you use in each exercise with a certified strength and conditioning specialist knowledgeable in tennis. Remember that you are not training to be a bodybuilder. Your goal is to play successful and injury-free tennis. Therefore, exercise technique is very important. The medicine ball chest throw (page 78) and supine medicine ball chest throw (page 79) provide an added benefit; you can easily mimic the movement pattern of the strokes, making each exercise tennis specific. Considered multijoint exercises, the medicine ball exercises involve other body parts to help with coordination and stability during the execution.

Push-Up

Triceps brachii

Anterior deltoid

Pectoralis major

Pectoralis minor

Execution

1. Assume a horizontal plank position with the head, shoulders, back, hips, knees, and feet in a straight line. The arms are extended and the palms are flat on the floor, with hands shoulder-width apart. Keep the feet together, supporting the weight of the lower body on the toes.

2. Inhale and slowly bend the elbows to bring the torso near the floor. Keep a neutral spine to prevent hyperextension (swayback).

3. At the bottom of the movement, contract the chest muscles and triceps to extend the arms, exhaling as the body rises. Repeat.

Muscles Involved

Primary: Pectoralis major, pectoralis minor

Secondary: Anterior deltoid, triceps brachii

Tennis Focus

The push-up is a great general exercise, but it has some specific tennis benefits as well. The muscles involved are activated in most tennis strokes but mostly in the forehand and serve. The backswing on the forehand stretches the muscles of the chest, while the acceleration and follow-through activate the concentric contractions of the chest muscles. Similar recruitment patterns occur on the serve, but the planes of motion are different; they are more vertical and less horizontal. Going very low in the push-up can put unnecessary strain on the anterior shoulder capsule and could result in impingement-related pain and discomfort. Limit the downward motion to a 90-degree angle at the elbow and shoulder to prevent shoulder injuries.

VARIATION

Changing the foot position of the push-up will isolate different aspects of the chest:

- Elevate the feet on a weight bench to isolate the upper pectorals and increase the difficulty of the exercise.
- Elevate the torso and place the hands on a weight bench to focus on the lower pectorals. This also decreases the difficulty of the exercise by lowering the amount of body weight used in the exercise.

Changing the hand position of the push-up will isolate different aspects of the chest:

- The diamond hand position increases the difficulty and recruits the triceps to a greater extent. Assume a push-up position, and place your hands so your index fingers and thumbs touch to form a diamond shape.
- The wide hand position decreases the difficulty and recruits the anterior deltoid, biceps, and pectorals to a greater extent. The wide hand position is similar to a traditional push-up position, but each hand is shifted 6 to 12 inches (15 to 30 cm) away from the body to increase the total distance between the hands.

Other variations involve performing push-ups on an unstable surface such as a medicine ball, BOSU ball, air pad, or weight bench.

Standing Alternate-Band Chest Press

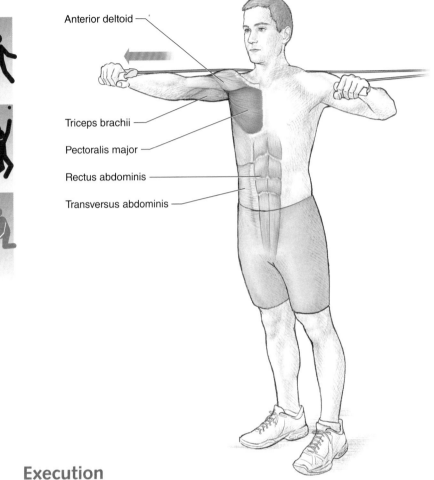

Anterior deltoid

Triceps brachii

Pectoralis major

Rectus abdominis

Transversus abdominis

Execution

1. Attach resistance tubing to a stable object. Stand upright with your feet shoulder-width apart and your core and lower body very stable. With your back to the tubing attachment, grip the handles of the tubing, one handle in each hand. Step away from the resistance. Hold your elbows out to the sides at shoulder height.

2. Slowly extend the right arm in front of the body by contracting the chest muscles and straightening the elbow. Hold the end position for one or two seconds.

3. Slowly return the right arm to the starting position. Repeat the movement with the left arm.

Muscles Involved

Primary: Pectoralis major, pectoralis minor

Secondary: Anterior deltoid, triceps brachii, rectus abdominis, transversus abdominis, erector spinae, multifidus

Tennis Focus

Since the standing alternate-band chest press does not involve a machine, it recruits several different muscles to provide muscular balance, including the muscles of the rotator cuff, shoulder, and upper back in addition to the chest muscles. When you use resistance tubing or a resistance band from a standing position, the stabilizing muscles of the core, upper back, and shoulders must actively contract to maintain good body position. This muscle use is in addition to the use of the prime movers of the chest. Although the forehand and

serve will benefit most from this exercise, the muscles activated assist in the acceleration and deceleration components of all strokes. An additional benefit is that resistance tubing is easy to carry when traveling. The movement pattern described is beneficial not only because it is a multijoint exercise but also because it involves the same muscles used in forehands and serves. This makes the exercise both practical and tennis specific. Because the exercise is conducted at a slower pace than the actual strokes, it is very safe as well.

VARIATION

TRX Suspension Trainer Chest Press

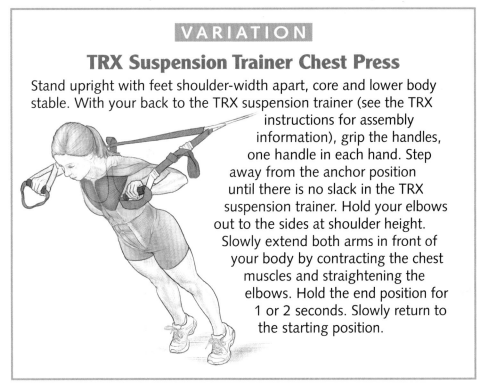

Stand upright with feet shoulder-width apart, core and lower body stable. With your back to the TRX suspension trainer (see the TRX instructions for assembly information), grip the handles, one handle in each hand. Step away from the anchor position until there is no slack in the TRX suspension trainer. Hold your elbows out to the sides at shoulder height. Slowly extend both arms in front of your body by contracting the chest muscles and straightening the elbows. Hold the end position for 1 or 2 seconds. Slowly return to the starting position.

Bench Press

Anterior deltoid

Pectoralis major

Serratus anterior

Triceps brachii

Execution

1. Lie on a weight bench with your back flat against the bench and your feet flat on the floor. Using a shoulder-width grip, grasp a barbell. Lift the bar and extend your arms straight out, keeping your hands above your eyes.

2. From this top position, slowly lower the bar by bending at the elbows. Eccentrically contract the chest muscles and the muscles around the front of the shoulders. Lower the bar under control until it gently touches the middle of the chest.

3. Immediately exhale and push the bar straight up by concentrically contracting the chest muscles until the elbows are straight but not locked. Repeat.

Muscles Involved

Primary: Pectoralis major, pectoralis minor, serratus anterior

Secondary: Anterior deltoid, triceps brachii

Tennis Focus

Volleys typically require a pushing or pressing motion similar to the bench press, medicine ball chest throw, and other related exercises. Pressing movements such as the bench press help develop both concentric and eccentric strength. The volley is a short punchlike swing that relies on the chest muscles, especially the pectoralis major and serratus anterior. The bench press is a slower, controlled version of the volley action and will help improve performance of this stroke and prevent injuries. Maintaining good pressing strength is important to protect other upper body muscles during all tennis strokes. Pressing strength is especially necessary when you have to hit a stroke while out of position or hit a very high ball. In these strokes, the lower body sometimes cannot generate as much force as desired, requiring the upper body to contribute more than usual.

VARIATION

Dumbbell Bench Press

Performing this exercise with two dumbbells instead of a barbell requires greater single-arm control. This will result in greater recruitment of stabilizing muscles around the shoulders. If you use dumbbells, you also can vary the hand position. The traditional grip, a pronated grip with the palms turned forward, provides more of a stretch as the weight is lowered to the chest. A neutral grip, with the palms turned toward each other, results in greater triceps recruitment.

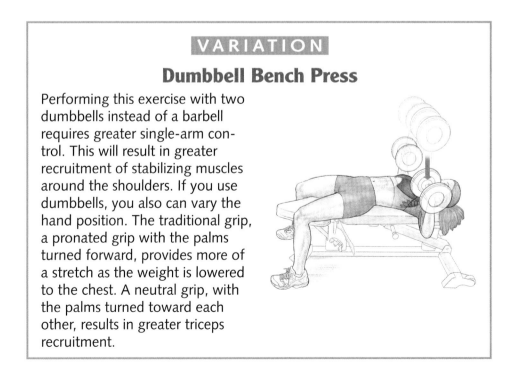

Incline Bench Press

Anterior deltoid

Triceps brachii

Upper pectoralis major

Pectoralis minor

Execution

1. Sit on an incline bench at a 30- to 35-degree incline, with feet firmly planted on the floor and back against the bench. While maintaining a stable core and lower body, grasp the bar using a shoulder-width grip.

2. Lift the barbell to start the movement. Extend the arms straight up above your eyes, straightening your arms but not locking the elbows. From this top position, slowly lower the bar by bending the elbows and eccentrically contracting the chest muscles and muscles around the front of the shoulders. Lower the bar under control until it gently touches the middle of the chest.

3. Immediately exhale and push the bar straight up by concentrically contracting the chest and anterior shoulder muscles until the elbows are straight but not locked. Repeat.

Muscles Involved

Primary: Upper pectoralis major, pectoralis minor

Secondary: Anterior deltoid, triceps brachii

Tennis Focus

The incline bench press is particularly beneficial to the muscles involved in serves, overheads, and forehands. It also helps develop the strength necessary to hit high balls effectively. This is beneficial when playing against players who impart heavy spin on the ball or when playing on surfaces that produce a high bounce. When an athlete is out of position, often the strength of the chest and shoulder contributes to the success of the stroke. Developing strength in the upper chest and anterior shoulder through exercises such as the incline bench press will allow greater force production in traditionally challenging positions for players. Specifically, it will aid the serve by improving overall muscular strength at and above eye level. This is an area that most tennis players do not train often and is typically an area that needs development.

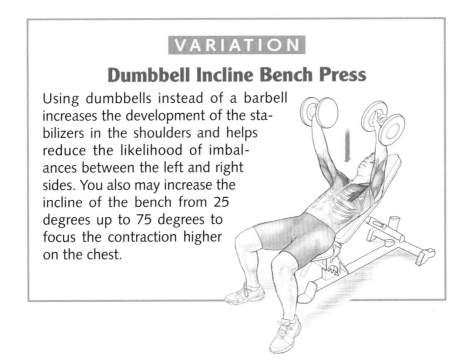

VARIATION

Dumbbell Incline Bench Press

Using dumbbells instead of a barbell increases the development of the stabilizers in the shoulders and helps reduce the likelihood of imbalances between the left and right sides. You also may increase the incline of the bench from 25 degrees up to 75 degrees to focus the contraction higher on the chest.

Medicine Ball Chest Throw

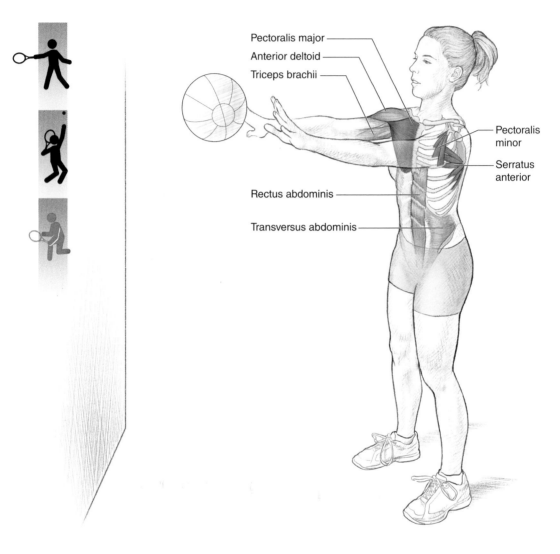

Pectoralis major
Anterior deltoid
Triceps brachii

Pectoralis minor

Serratus anterior

Rectus abdominis

Transversus abdominis

Execution

1. Choose a moderately heavy medicine ball. One that is 6 to 20 pounds (2.5 to 9 kg) is good for this exercise. Take into account your strength, age, and any contraindications when choosing a ball.

2. Stand in an athletic position with your feet shoulder-width apart, knees slightly bent, and core contracted. Face a solid wall. Hold the medicine ball in both hands. Start with your arms extended in front of your chest.

3. Explosively bend your elbows to bring the medicine ball to your chest, and then rapidly throw the ball against the wall by contracting your chest and triceps muscles. Retrieve the ball and repeat.

Muscles Involved

Primary: Pectoralis major, pectoralis minor, serratus anterior

Secondary: Anterior deltoid, triceps brachii, rectus abdominis, transversus abdominis, erector spinae, multifidus

Tennis Focus

The medicine ball chest throw is an excellent exercise that requires only a medicine ball. The main focus is on the pectoralis major, triceps, and serratus anterior. These muscles are particularly engaged during the upward or forward swing of the tennis serve in addition to most other strokes. The secondary muscles provide stability and balance during this exercise, similar to the stability and balance they would provide during the service motion.

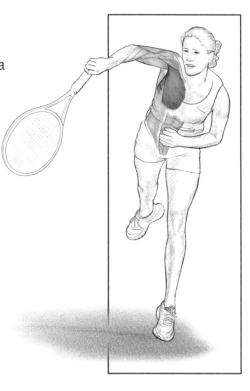

VARIATION

Supine Medicine Ball Chest Throw

The medicine ball chest throw is an explosive upper body plyometric movement. To increase the difficulty, have a partner or coach help you try this variation. Lie on the ground on your back. Bend your knees, and plant your heels flat on the floor. Extend your arms straight up in front of your eyes, grasping a light medicine ball (4 to 8 pounds [1.8 to 3.63 kg]). Bend your elbows, bringing the medicine ball to your chest. When the medicine ball touches your chest, rapidly throw the ball as high as possible over your eyes, making sure your partner is there to catch it. After catching the ball, your partner gently drops the ball over your chest. Catch the medicine ball by eccentrically contracting the chest muscles. After catching the ball, immediately attempt to throw it up again. Focus on producing explosive power from the upper body.

Dumbbell Chest Fly

Biceps brachii

Anterior deltoid

Coracobrachialis

Pectoralis major

Execution

1. Lie on a flat weight bench with your back flat against the bench and feet flat against the floor. Grasp a dumbbell in each hand. Use a neutral grip, palms turned toward each other. Extend your arms over your chest, elbows slightly bent.
2. Slowly lower the dumbbells to the sides, slightly bending your elbows, until your elbows are just below shoulder height.
3. Raise the dumbbells by contracting the chest muscles to return to the starting position, and repeat.

Muscles Involved

Primary: Pectoralis major

Secondary: Anterior deltoid, coracobrachialis, biceps brachii

Tennis Focus

The dumbbell chest fly is a great exercise to prepare you for the forehand groundstroke. The modern forehand groundstroke is hit from an open stance and with a very forceful swing. Therefore, the muscles required have to be strong but also able to resist fatigue so you can perform throughout a long match. Using dumbbells for this exercise instead of a machine forces the secondary muscles to provide stability and balance. This exercise also will help limit the likelihood of injury on a wide forehand groundstroke or when your base of support is wider than normal. The chest and arm are required to be stretched to a greater degree while still maintaining force output.

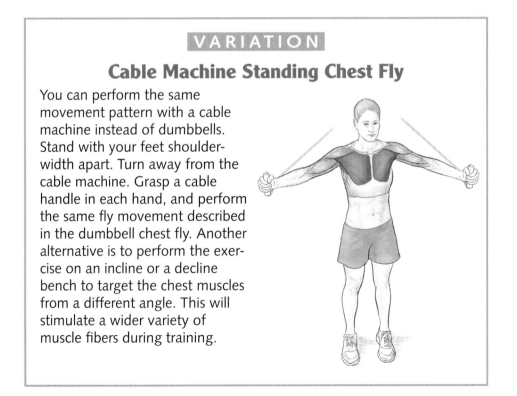

VARIATION

Cable Machine Standing Chest Fly

You can perform the same movement pattern with a cable machine instead of dumbbells. Stand with your feet shoulder-width apart. Turn away from the cable machine. Grasp a cable handle in each hand, and perform the same fly movement described in the dumbbell chest fly. Another alternative is to perform the exercise on an incline or a decline bench to target the chest muscles from a different angle. This will stimulate a wider variety of muscle fibers during training.

You must not overlook the muscles of the back when training for tennis performance and injury prevention. Although these muscles do act concentrically, particularly during the backhand stroke, we cannot overlook the importance of the eccentric action of these muscles, especially during the follow-through phases of the serve and forehand stroke. A strong back will encourage correct posture, create balance between dominant and nondominant sides of the body, protect the surrounding joints, and serve as a link between the lower and upper body. Since in tennis the back must provide flexion, extension, and rotation, a well-developed upper and lower back is crucial for optimal performance on the court.

As mentioned in chapter 4, some muscles wrap around and can be labeled as either back (posterior) or chest (anterior) muscles. The pectoralis minor and serratus anterior, for example, are highlighted in chapter 4, although they also serve a supporting role in some of the exercises in this chapter.

Back Anatomy

The muscles of the back provide flexibility and mobility of the spine and, when trained correctly, promote good posture. Generally the deeper muscles act to support and move the spine, while the more superficial muscles move the arms and shoulders. The deep muscles are built in layers. There are numerous muscles in these layers, but for the purposes of this chapter, we will focus only on the major muscles and the muscles covered in the exercises.

Many back muscles are typically described as shoulder muscles; however, because of their critical interplay with the back, they deserve mention here. The rotator cuff (see figure 2.1, page 24) is made up of four short muscles: the subscapularis, supraspinatus, infraspinatus, and teres minor. These muscles attach to and strengthen the joint capsule and maintain the humerus in the joint socket. They are vitally important for the stability of the shoulder joint. The deltoid muscle (see figure 2.2, page 24) gives the shoulder its rounded appearance and is the prime mover for raising the arm in front or to the side of the body.

In the upper back (figure 5.1, page 84), the trapezius attaches to the skull and helps hold up and rotate the head. It also works in concert with the levator scapulae to move the scapula up and in toward the midline of the body. The latissimus dorsi is the largest and most powerful back muscle. (*Latissimus* means *broadest* in Latin.) This muscle is attached to the spine from above the lower edge of the trapezius and runs down to the back of the pelvis. It helps pull the arm (humerus) down toward the midline of the body and also assists in pulling the shoulders back.

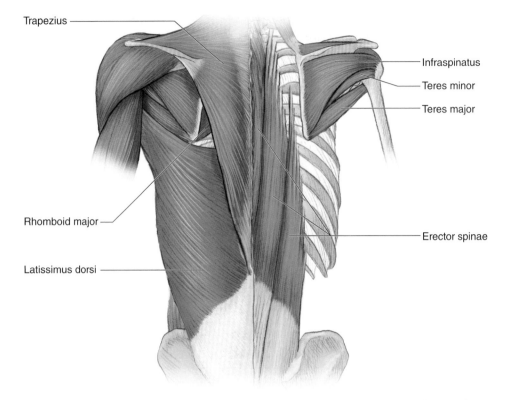

Figure 5.1 Muscles of the back: trapezius, rhomboid major, latissimus dorsi, infraspinatus, teres minor, teres major, and erector spinae.

This is the major muscle that provides the visual V-taper silhouette. The rhomboids (major and minor) run between the spine and scapula and move the scapula up and in (retraction). The rhomboids are the major muscles involved in squeezing the shoulder blades together. The main muscle that provides the opposite action (protraction) is the serratus anterior, which wraps itself around the wall of the rib cage to attach to the scapula's inner edge. The erector spinae muscle group makes up the outer layer of back muscles. The erector spinae stabilize the spine and help you maintain an erect posture or extend the spine.

Two important muscle groups in the lower back include the multifidus and quadratus lumborum (figure 5.2), which

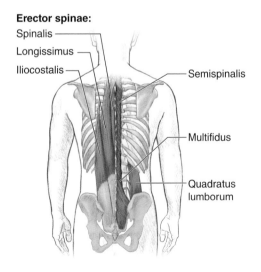

Figure 5.2 Multifidus and quadratus lumborum.

are important for spine stability. Also important, particularly for tennis players, is the psoas major, which connects the lumbar spine to the hip flexors.

Tennis Strokes and Back Movement

During the serve, the loading phase (backswing) puts the back into a hyperextended and rotated position. This position puts a lot of stress on the muscles and the surrounding joints of the back. This is a major reason to strengthen both upper and lower back muscles. Tennis is a sport of emergencies. There are frequent stops and starts, lunges for balls almost out of reach, and changes of direction several times per point. All of these motions place heavy demands on the body, especially the back. Combine this with the fact that many players neglect to train the back, at least to the same extent as the muscles in the front of the body, and you can see how players set themselves up for injuries or poor performance. The exercises outlined in this chapter help strengthen the back muscles, with a particular focus on those muscles involved in the follow-through of the serve and forehand and the muscles that are the prime movers of the one- and two-handed backhand in the acceleration (forward) swing. Because the back is critical in transferring forces from the lower to the upper body as part of the kinetic chain, rotational exercises are also recommended and included.

Exercises for the Back

Back exercises should be done regularly. Muscular balance is very important for tennis players. Since the muscles on the front of the body—the chest and front of the shoulder—are typically stronger in tennis players because of the repeated actions of these body parts during the strokes, the back musculature requires particular attention. Perform back exercises several times a week, with a day of rest in between sessions. Proper technique is very important; therefore, we recommend consulting a certified strength and conditioning specialist who is knowledgeable in tennis. When using equipment, perform two or three sets of 10 to 12 repetitions. Many exercises can be performed using your own body weight or with medicine balls. Medicine ball exercises are full-body exercises that incorporate rotational movements and so are very tennis specific. Even though tennis often requires the back muscles to act eccentrically, we recommend starting a strength and conditioning program for the back with concentric exercises to develop a strong baseline of strength. A strength and conditioning coach can tell you when to start incorporating eccentric strength exercises into your individual program.

Lat Pull-Down

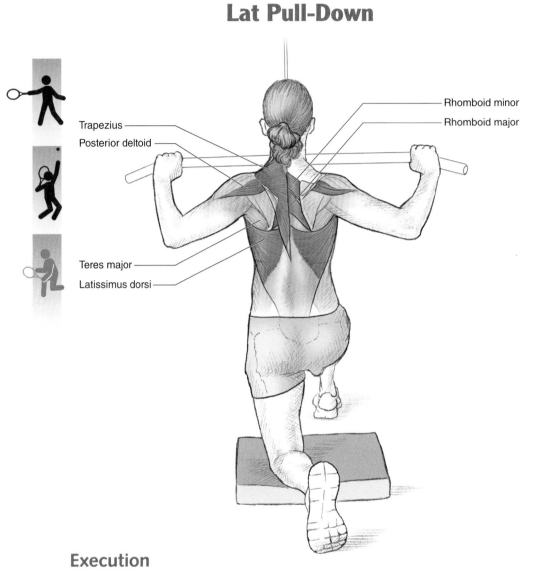

Rhomboid minor

Rhomboid major

Trapezius

Posterior deltoid

Teres major

Latissimus dorsi

Execution

1. Kneel on a mat, facing a cable machine. Grab the bar with your hands slightly wider than shoulder-width apart, palms facing out. Establish a stable core.

2. Pull the bar down in front of your head to approximately the level of the breastbone (sternum). Focus on squeezing your shoulder blades together.

3. Slowly return to the starting position and repeat.

Muscles Involved

Primary: Latissimus dorsi, trapezius, posterior deltoid, rhomboid major, rhomboid minor

Secondary: Biceps brachii, teres major

Tennis Focus

The muscles involved in this exercise serve an important role in protecting the upper back and shoulder joint by providing eccentric strength in the follow-through phases of the serve and the forehand. Retraction of the shoulder blades helps strengthen the muscles protecting the scapulae. These are very important muscles for tennis players. They are also responsible for the loading phase of the serve. The largest muscle groups of the back are included in this exercise. The latissimus dorsi is the largest and most powerful muscle in the back and provides both concentric and eccentric contractions during the tennis strokes.

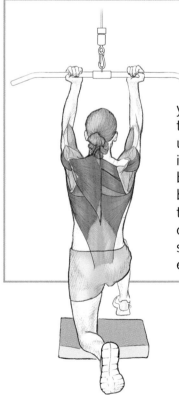

VARIATION

Chin-Up

If you place your hands closer, about 2 or 3 inches (5 to 8 cm) apart, and turn your palms to face inward in a chin-up position, you will place a greater focus on the scapular stabilizers. Be sure to pull the bar down in front of the head; pulling the weight down behind the head places unnecessary stress on both the joint and the scapular stabilizers. Pull the weight down to the upper part of your chest while simultaneously pushing your chest slightly out and up. You also can perform this exercise in a lat pull-down machine.

Rotational Pull

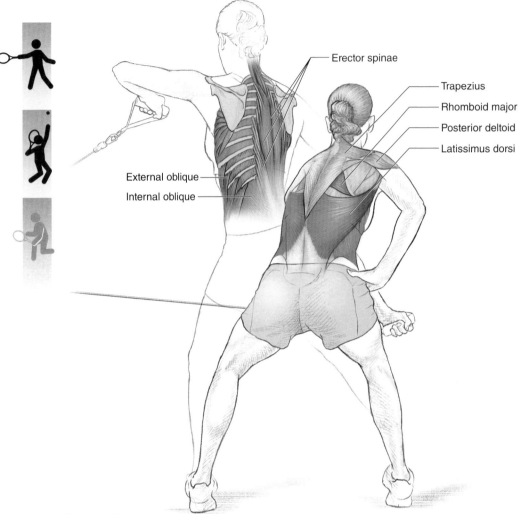

Erector spinae

Trapezius

Rhomboid major

Posterior deltoid

Latissimus dorsi

External oblique

Internal oblique

Execution

1. On a cable pulley machine, set the cable height to about hip height. Grasp the handle with your left hand on the outside of your right foot while standing in an athletic position beside the cable machine. (In an athletic position, your weight is evenly distributed between your feet, knees are slightly bent, back is straight, head is up, and eyes are forward.) Maintain good balance as you lean forward slightly, mimicking the ready position.

2. While maintaining an athletic position, pull the cable so that your left elbow comes up to the level of your left shoulder via contractions of your upper back muscles. Move slowly and under control while focusing on squeezing your shoulder blades together.

3. After completing the repetitions on your left arm, switch arms and perform the same motion using the right arm.

Muscles Involved

Primary: Rhomboid major, rhomboid minor, internal oblique, external oblique, erector spinae, latissimus dorsi

Secondary: Posterior deltoid, trapezius

Tennis Focus

The upper back is vital during all deceleration aspects of tennis strokes. These back muscles need to be trained in a single plane of motion as well as in rotational planes of motion. Rotations are vitally important in the modern tennis game. Both forehand and backhand groundstrokes and the serve require significant body rotations to create forceful shots. Both upper and lower back musculature improves by incorporating this exercise into an overall program. A comprehensive training program should focus not just on flexion and extension exercises but also on the development of the back muscles in rotational directions to help strengthen the muscles needed to protect the shoulder and help slow down the racket and upper body after ball contact.

VARIATION

Medicine Ball Handoff

If a cable pulley machine is not available, this exercise can be replicated using a medicine ball. Two players stand back to back. As they rotate, they hand the medicine ball off to each other. Make sure each player gets to rotate in each direction.

Seated Row

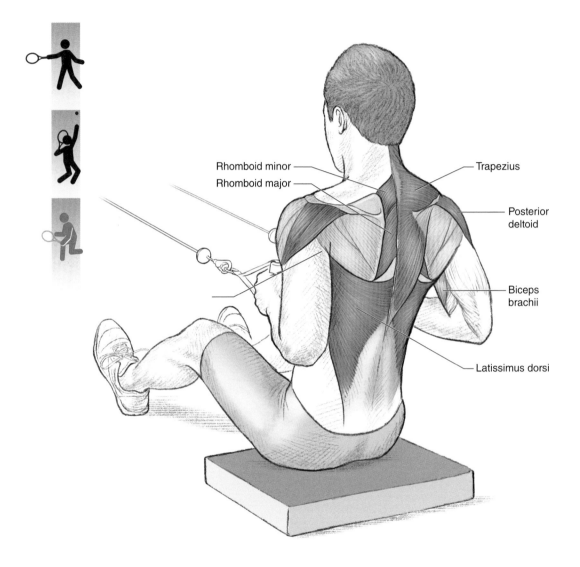

Rhomboid minor
Rhomboid major
Trapezius
Posterior deltoid
Biceps brachii
Latissimus dorsi

Execution

1. Sit facing a cable machine set close to the floor, or use a seated row machine if one is available. Grab the handles at about chest height.
2. Pull the handles toward you as you squeeze the shoulder blades together (retraction). Maintain a stable core.
3. Slowly release the weight back to the starting position and repeat.

Muscles Involved

Primary: Trapezius, rhomboid major, rhomboid minor, latissimus dorsi, posterior deltoid

Secondary: Biceps brachii

Tennis Focus

This may be the single most important upper body exercise for tennis players. The muscles involved in this exercise, including the scapular stabilizers, need to be strengthened to help protect the shoulders and upper back. With the way serves and forehands in particular are hit, the muscles developed during this exercise work eccentrically to help protect the shoulder and upper back, especially during the follow-through after ball contact. In addition, these muscles are crucially important during the backhand stroke since they provide the strength (through a concentric contraction) for the forward swing. Developing good rhomboid and scapular retraction control through this exercise will improve body posture and reduce the likelihood of the overdevelopment of the trapezius, which can result in neck pain and greater chance of injury.

VARIATION

Standing Row

This exercise can be completed from a standing position as well. In addition, it can be performed from a seated position, but as the weight is pulled back, the elbows are kept at shoulder level, allowing for significant involvement of the posterior deltoid.

Reverse Fly

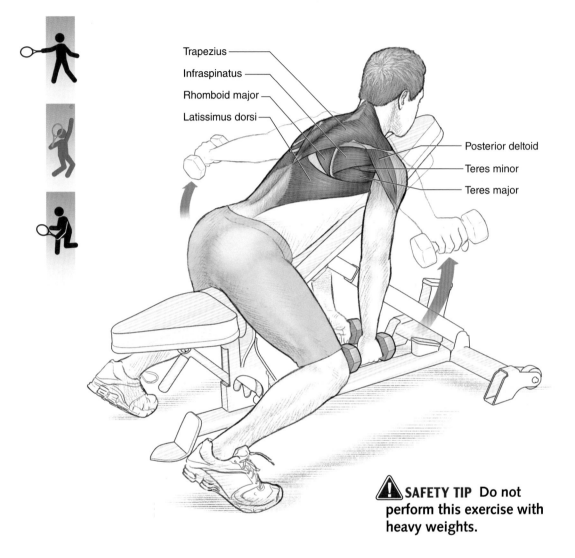

Trapezius

Infraspinatus

Rhomboid major

Latissimus dorsi

Posterior deltoid

Teres minor

Teres major

⚠ **SAFETY TIP** Do not perform this exercise with heavy weights.

Execution

1. Lie facedown on an incline bench set at a 45- to 60-degree incline. Hold a dumbbell in each hand. The arms should be extended or minimally flexed at the elbows. Palms are facing inward.

2. Raise the elbows to shoulder level, keeping the palms down.

3. Slowly lower to the starting position.

Muscles Involved

Primary: Posterior deltoid, rhomboid major, rhomboid minor, trapezius, latissimus dorsi, teres major, teres minor, infraspinatus

Secondary: Brachialis, biceps brachii

Tennis Focus

This exercise focuses on those muscles that help protect the shoulder girdle. They are particularly active during the contact and deceleration of the backhand volley stroke. The goal is to strengthen the scapular stabilizers by contracting the surrounding muscle groups. This exercise should be performed with light weights since the objective is to work on muscular endurance while maintaining proper technique. Much of what happens during a tennis match is very similar to this exercise in that players will have to perform many backhands over the length of a match. The reverse fly allows players to strengthen the appropriate muscles to improve muscular endurance during long matches.

Bent-Over Row

Trapezius

Posterior deltoid

Rhomboid major

Latissimus dorsi

Execution

1. Stand with your feet about shoulder-width apart, knees slightly bent (approximately 30-degree knee flexion). As you maintain a stable core, reach down and grasp a barbell with both hands slightly wider than shoulder-width apart. Do not round your back. Lift the barbell to knee height.

2. From this starting position, squeeze your shoulder blades together, and contract your rhomboids and latissimus dorsi to pull the bar toward your chest while maintaining a stable core and lower body.

3. Slowly return to the starting position and repeat.

Muscles Involved

Primary: Posterior deltoid, rhomboid major, rhomboid minor, latissimus dorsi

Secondary: Trapezius, erector spinae

Tennis Focus

The purpose of the bent-over row is to improve the strength of the scapular stabilizers and back muscles. In addition, similar to the lat pull-down exercise, this is an excellent exercise to promote muscular balance between dominant and nondominant sides of the body. These muscles act eccentrically in the follow-through phase of both the serve and forehand, and they are also involved in the concentric phase (forward swing) of the backhand stroke. The bent-over row also helps develop core stability.

VARIATION

Dumbbell Row

This exercise can also be performed using dumbbells instead of a barbell.

Deadlift

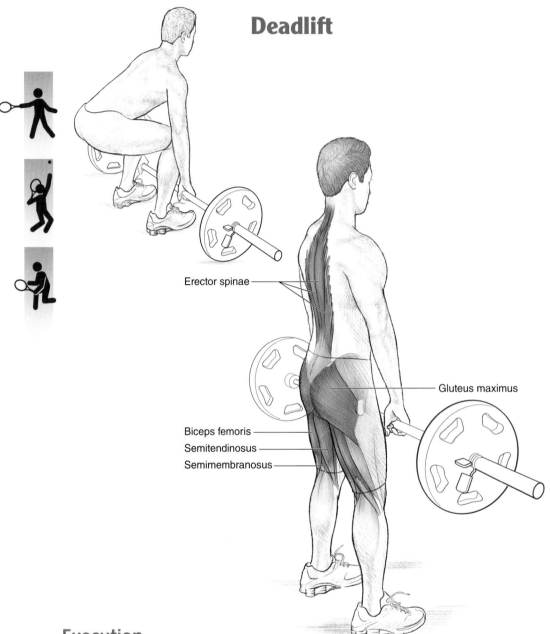

Erector spinae

Gluteus maximus

Biceps femoris
Semitendinosus
Semimembranosus

Execution

1. Place a barbell on the ground or a lifting platform. Stand with your feet approximately shoulder-width apart. Grab the bar using an overhand grip, hands at least shoulder-width apart, and squat down so your hips are near parallel to your knees. Squeeze your shoulder blades together.

2. Contract your hip extensors and stand upright, lifting the bar to hip level while keeping the arms extended.

3. Flex the knees and lower the weight, under control, back to the floor to return to the starting position.

Muscles Involved

Primary: Gluteus maximus, biceps femoris, semimembranosus, semitendinosus, erector spinae

Secondary: Psoas major, multifidus, quadratus lumborum, latissimus dorsi, trapezius

Tennis Focus

One of the most frequently injured areas of the body is the lower back. This exercise works on a number of different areas of the body, including the trapezius and hips, but the main focus is the lower back. A strong lower back is very important because the back is the link between the upper and lower body. Forces produced in the lower body have to be transferred through a strong back to the trunk and arm and ultimately the racket and ball. This transfer of forces can clearly be seen in the service motion. The lifting (upward) phase of the deadlift develops strength through a movement similar to the one used to come out of the knee bend on the serve.

> ### VARIATION
> ## Over–Under Grip
> To work with a heavier weight or to keep the weight from rolling off your hands, use an over–under grip. Grab the bar with one palm turned toward you and the other turned away from you.

CORE AND TORSO

A tennis player has a top and bottom half, a left and right side, and a front and back side. The core, or torso, connects each of these areas to the rest of the body and therefore might be the most important section of the body to train properly. The core includes several larger muscle groups that are involved in movement in each of the planes of motion. In the modern tennis game, rotational movements in particular have become more common, and tennis players need to take a three-dimensional view to training in order to develop a balanced program. Simply performing a few sit-ups or crunches does not prepare the body for the rotational, lateral, hyperextension, and flexion movements required to successfully compete at a recreational or competitive level. The core serves as an important component in the summation of forces initially generated from the ground and transferred up through the rest of the body to the racket and ball. The focus of tennis-specific exercises for the core should be on stability, balance, posture, performance enhancement, and injury prevention.

Core Anatomy

The anatomy of the core is focused on the center of the body. The core is made up of muscle groups in the front, back, and sides of the body as well as muscles that wrap around the body.

The erector spinae (figure 6.1a, page 100) runs along the spine and controls forward flexion. It helps maintain an upright posture. It is actually made up of several muscles and extends throughout the lumbar, thoracic, and cervical regions. Both the quadratus lumborum and the multifidus are two deep muscle groups that help with spine stability and lateral flexion.

The psoas major is sometimes referred to as the iliopsoas, which technically is a combination of the iliacus and psoas major muscles (figure 6.1b, page 100). It connects the lumbar spine to the hip flexors. The iliacus is important for flexing the leg forward. However, both the iliacus and psoas major also bend the trunk forward and can lift the trunk from a lying posture (as in sit-ups) because the psoas major crosses several vertebral joints and the sacroiliac joint.

The rectus abdominis (figure 6.2, page 100) is composed of two straplike muscles that run vertically. It extends along the front of the abdomen. This is the muscle typically seen as the six pack in highly trained athletes. The rectus abdominis originates at the front of the rib cage and inserts at the pelvis. The transversus abdominis lies deeper, under the rectus abdominis. The transversus abdominis wraps around the body, almost like a natural belt, and its fibers run horizontally.

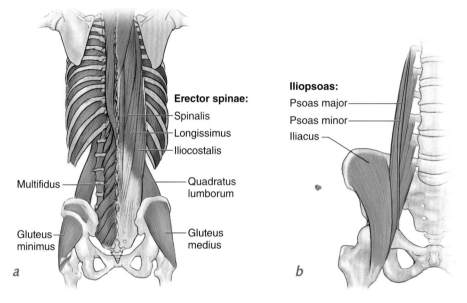

Figure 6.1   Core muscles on the *(a)* back and *(b)* front of the body.

It is critical in stabilizing the pelvis and supporting the torso. Both the transversus abdominis and internal oblique muscles lie below the external oblique muscles. The internal oblique is a broad, thin sheet. Its fibers run up and in at approximately 90 degrees to the external oblique. The obliques assist in rotating the trunk.

The serratus anterior (discussed in chapters 4 and 5 as well) is an eight-part muscle that pulls the scapula forward (protraction). It also helps in stabilizing the scapula. It originates on the surface of the upper eight or nine ribs at the side of the chest and inserts along the entire anterior length of the medial border of the scapula.

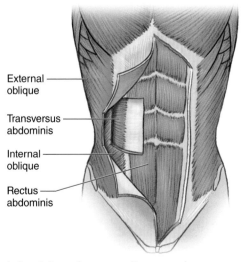

Figure 6.2   Rectus abdominis and surrounding muscles.

Tennis Strokes and Core Movement

Tennis players today frequently hit groundstrokes from an open stance. An open stance requires the body to rotate in a transverse, or horizontal, plane. In the loading (backswing) phase of the stroke, the muscles of the midsection, or core, are stretched so this stored potential elastic energy can be released as kinetic energy in the acceleration (forward) phase of the stroke. Proper preparation of the core is a must in helping to prevent injury and create a better performance on the court. Remember, many of these muscles also transfer forces from the lower to upper body in the kinetic chain. Training should include the muscles of the back, front, and sides of the body—a balanced program, in other words. A properly balanced program will help with posture, stability, and body control in extreme positions. The trunk and core are involved in each and every one of the tennis strokes; therefore, strengthening these muscles is more important than strengthening any others.

Exercises for the Core

Many players are taught to do sit-ups daily as part of their training. For tennis players, there is nothing wrong with performing sit-ups, crunches, or any other exercises beneficial for the abdominals. However, it is more important to create proper balance. Be sure to include exercises for the front and back as well as the muscles responsible for rotating the body. Performing these exercises at least every other day with a day of rest in between will be a big help in your performance as well as injury prevention. Many of these exercises can be performed without the use of equipment. Your own body weight provides the resistance. If more resistance is needed, use a medicine ball or another form of weighted resistance such as dumbbells, weight plates, or sandbags. Since these are some of the larger muscle groups of the body, they provide balance and stability. Speed is not much of an issue when you are performing these exercises. Perform them with proper technique, and make sure you work all sides of the core.

Crunch

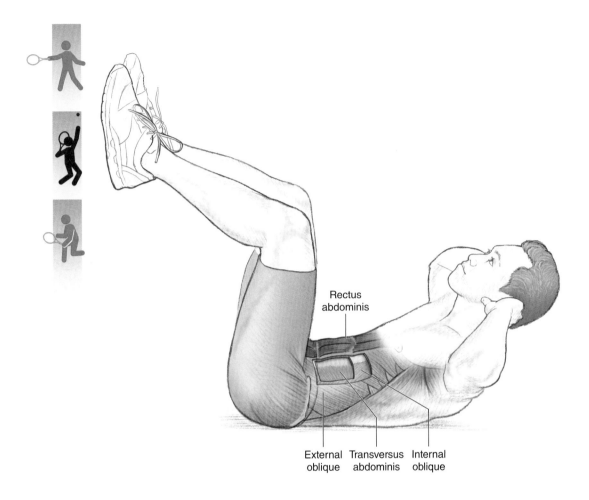

Rectus
abdominis

External   Transversus   Internal
oblique   abdominis   oblique

Execution

1. Lie flat on the floor, hips and knees bent at 90 degrees and feet off the floor, with hands touching your ears.

2. Raise your shoulders and upper back off the floor, bringing your chest forward by firmly contracting your abdominals while keeping your lower back in contact with the floor. Focus on contracting your core muscles to initiate body movement. Do not pull on your neck with your hands to initiate movement.

3. Slowly lower your upper back and shoulders to the starting position and repeat.

Muscles Involved

Primary: Rectus abdominis

Secondary: Transversus abdominis, internal oblique, external oblique

Tennis Focus

During all tennis strokes, the core muscles contract and relax at different points throughout the movement to help improve performance and reduce the chance of injury. The rectus abdominis contracts during contact on the serve and is involved as a secondary muscle at contact during groundstrokes and volleys. The muscles of the core also play a vital role in stabilizing the body, especially during the deceleration portions of all strokes, including the serve.

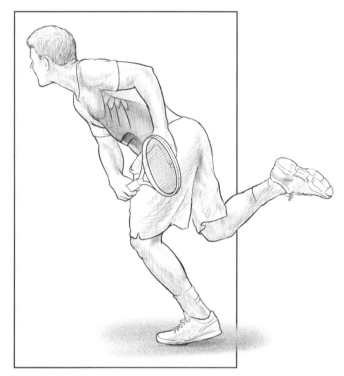

VARIATION

Reverse Crunch

The reverse crunch has the same starting position. Instead of raising the shoulders and upper back off the floor, raise the pelvis off the floor by firmly contracting the rectus abdominis and hip flexors (iliopsoas and rectus femoris), and secondarily the obliques. The reverse crunch aids the development of the lower portion of the core and hip flexors, an area many tennis players rely on to maintain a low center of mass during groundstrokes and volleys. Injuries are rather common in this region, and the addition of the reverse crunch will help strengthen the muscles of the lower core.

Rotational Crunch

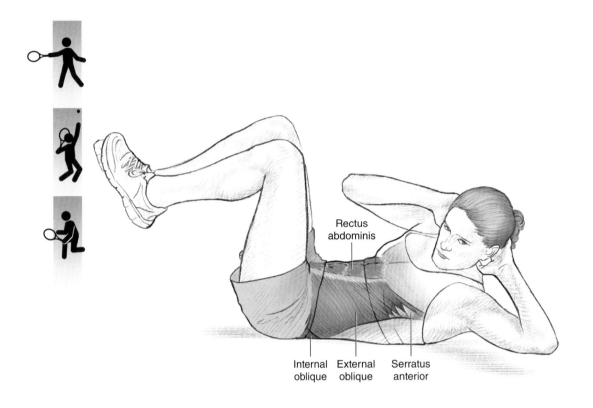

Rectus abdominis

Internal oblique   External oblique   Serratus anterior

Execution

1. Lie flat on the floor, hips and knees bent at 90 degrees and feet off the floor, with hands touching your ears.
2. As you initiate the sit-up movement and crunch, rotate your torso, moving your right elbow toward your left knee, trying to touch it.
3. Slowly return to the starting position. For the next repetition, direct your left elbow toward your right knee.

Muscles Involved

Primary: Internal oblique, external oblique, rectus abdominis

Secondary: Serratus anterior, iliacus, psoas major, transversus abdominis

Tennis Focus

The majority of movements in tennis rely on rotation in a transverse plane. Therefore, it is important to strengthen the muscles of the core in movement patterns similar to those performed during play. The internal and external obliques, along with the rectus abdominis, are the primary driving muscles. However, during both forehand and backhand groundstrokes and the serve, the rotational muscles of the core are highly active during the loading phase, when these muscles are pre-stretched, and again during the acceleration phase, when the stored energy created during the loading phase is released to accelerate the swing.

VARIATION

Bicycle

The bicycle requires the same starting position. As the right elbow moves toward the left knee, the right leg extends via a core contraction and hip extension. This movement is then repeated to the other side. This exercise can be performed slowly, at medium speed, or quickly.

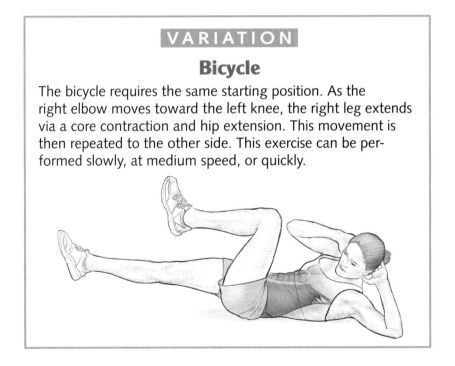

Toe Touch

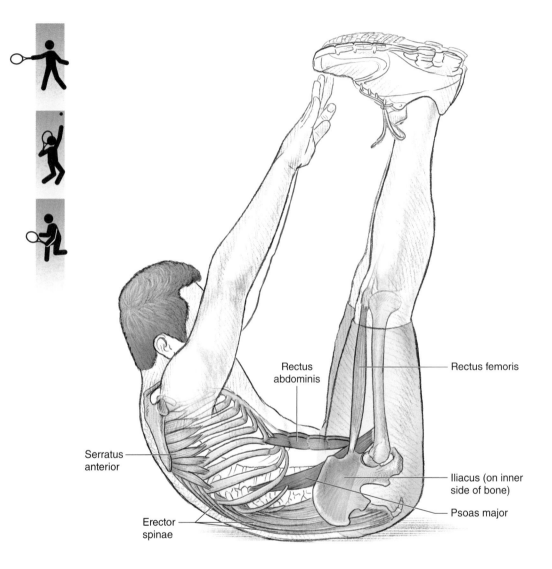

Rectus abdominis

Rectus femoris

Serratus anterior

Iliacus (on inner side of bone)

Psoas major

Erector spinae

Execution

1. Lie flat on the floor, hips bent at 90 degrees and legs straight, with heels pointing to the ceiling. Extend your arms straight above your eyes.

2. Using a core contraction to initiate the movement, raise your hands to touch your toes. Keep your feet straight in the air. Relax your neck.

3. While continuing to contract the abdominals, lower to the starting position and repeat.

Muscles Involved

Primary: Rectus abdominis, iliacus, psoas major

Secondary: Rectus femoris, transversus abdominis, serratus anterior, external oblique, multifidus, erector spinae

Tennis Focus

Hip flexor strength and hamstring flexibility are both important components of tennis. This exercise helps develop both of these physical components while also developing abdominal and lower back strength. Having good hip flexor strength is vital when loading the lower body on groundstrokes, volleys, and serves, and it is highly evident during the follow-through and landing phase of the lower body during the serve.

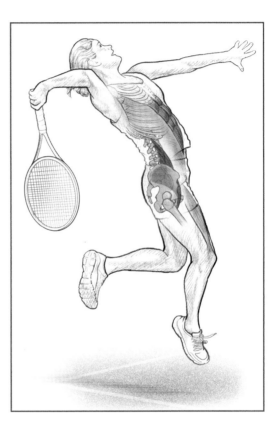

VARIATION

Rotational Toe Touch

Perform the same movement, but as you raise your hands to touch your toes, reach your left hand across your body to touch the outside of your right foot. Return to the starting position. Then reach your right hand across your body to touch your left foot. This movement results in greater involvement of the obliques and the serratus anterior.

Plank

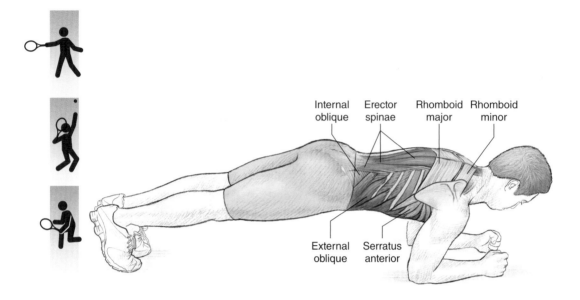

Execution

1. Lie facedown, with your elbows and forearms underneath you and in line with your shoulders. Your legs lie straight on the ground, with your feet, knees, and quadriceps touching the ground, feet approximately shoulder-width apart.

2. Lift yourself into a bridge position by contracting your core and hip muscles and pushing down on your forearms and toes. Raise your body from the ground until only the forearms and toes remain in contact with the ground.

3. Hold this position while maintaining a neutral spine (flat back). Beginners hold the position for 10 to 30 seconds; advanced athletes hold it for one to three minutes.

⚠️**SAFETY TIP** Do not let your hips and back sag. This exercise will be effective only if you maintain a flat line from your shoulders to your feet.

Muscles Involved

Primary: Transversus abdominis, rectus abdominis, internal oblique, external oblique, multifidus, erector spinae

Secondary: Iliacus, psoas major, serratus anterior, rhomboid major, rhomboid minor

Tennis Focus

Tennis is a dynamic sport in which all movements must use the stretch–shortening cycle. Although the plank is an isometric exercise that does not require the stretch–shortening cycle, it is still a very important training tool for tennis. The ability to stabilize the body to hit a wide ball, rotate the trunk during groundstrokes and serves, or make contact during volleys and overheads may be improved through the plank. The plank also is important for preventing injury to the core and hip muscles, areas at high risk of injury for tennis players. Continue to develop this exercise, and progress by increasing the difficulty through holding the position for longer periods or adding resistance, when appropriate.

VARIATION

Side Plank

The side plank is only one of many plank variations. For the side plank, lean on your right elbow in a side-lying position, with your shoulders and hips parallel to the floor. Place your left hand on the hip. The side-lying position greatly increases the muscle activation of the obliques, which are vital for improved stability through the core during rotational movements. Other variations include weighted planks and unbalanced planks. Weighted planks should be performed only after you have developed to the point of needing more resistance to keep adapting and growing. Unbalanced planks are performed on an unstable surface such as an exercise ball or BOSU ball and require greater stabilization and core contractions to maintain good posture.

Russian Twist

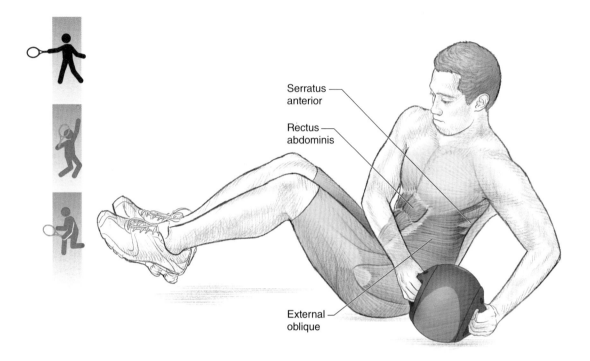

Serratus anterior

Rectus abdominis

External oblique

Execution

1. Sit on the floor, holding a medicine ball in both hands in front of your body, hips and knees bent at approximately 45 degrees to the shoulders. The upper back is at a 45-degree angle to the floor and forms a 90-degree angle with the upper legs. The feet are off the ground.
2. Rotate the trunk to the left so that the medicine ball touches the ground by your left hip.
3. Rotate the trunk back to the right so that the medicine ball touches the ground by your right hip. Repeat.

Muscles Involved

Primary: Rectus abdominis, internal oblique, external oblique

Secondary: Serratus anterior, iliacus, psoas major, transversus abdominis, multifidus

Tennis Focus

This exercise specifically focuses on the movement needed to execute groundstrokes, especially the loading phase of the back-swing on both the forehand and backhand groundstrokes. By vary-ing the speed of the rotations, this exercise also can help develop power in the muscles of the core in a rotational movement path. It can do the same when performed with slight resistance and when performed at rapid speed.

VARIATION

Exercise Ball Russian Twist

Lie on an exercise ball, with your feet on the ground and your shoul-ders and upper back on the ball. Rotate the trunk to the right, and feel the right oblique contract. Repeat the movement to the left. Since this exercise is a bit more unstable, it requires the involvement of more secondary muscles to maintain stability.

Swimmer

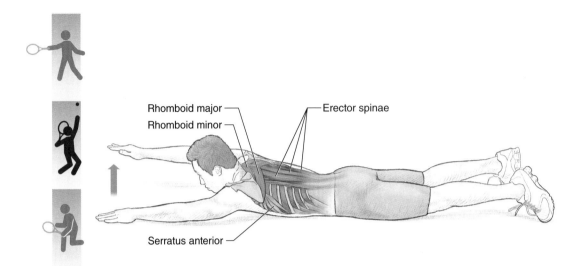

Execution

1. Lie facedown on the ground, with arms extended above your head.
2. While keeping your feet on the floor, lift your left arm up and down above your head by contracting the muscles in your lower and upper back and shoulder.
3. Switch arms, lifting the right arm up and down above your head.
4. Repeat this movement, alternating arms, for the duration of the exercise.

Muscles Involved

Primary: Erector spinae, multifidus, rhomboid major, rhomboid minor

Secondary: Latissimus dorsi, serratus anterior

Tennis Focus

The muscles of the lower back (erector spinae, multifidus) are heavily involved in most tennis movements. They are vital during deceleration after a groundstroke or serve. Their role during the serve is paramount. Most good servers have a separation angle of approximately 20 degrees between the shoulders and the hips during the loading phase of the serve. They also exhibit a vertical tilt (lateral flexion) of the trunk. Obtaining this effective serving position requires both strength and stability in the muscles of the lower back to prevent injuries and allow for efficient energy transfer to the ball.

VARIATION

Rotational Swimmer

Perform the same movement pattern as in the swimmer exercise, but instead of raising the arm up and down in a single plane, rotate the trunk and upper back slightly as the arm is raised. This will require greater muscle recruitment from the latissimus dorsi, obliques, and serratus anterior.

Prone Snow Angel

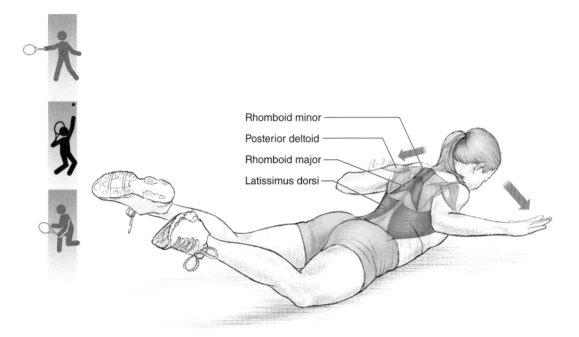

Rhomboid minor
Posterior deltoid
Rhomboid major
Latissimus dorsi

Execution

1. Lie facedown on the floor, with your hands touching above your head and your elbows bent at approximately 45 degrees. Your legs are extended and your feet are off the ground.

2. Lower your elbows toward your hips by squeezing your shoulder blades together. Maintain a 45-degree bend in the elbows. Raise the upper back, and keep the feet off the ground.

3. Return to the starting position and repeat.

Muscles Involved

Primary: Erector spinae, multifidus, rhomboid major, rhomboid minor, latissimus dorsi

Secondary: Posterior deltoid

Tennis Focus

This exercise is particularly important in protecting the upper and lower back from injury. The muscles that act eccentrically during the follow-through for both the serve and overhead are strengthened concentrically by this exercise, providing protection to the scapulae and the musculature of the lower back. Having good control of the upper back and shoulders is sometimes termed *scapular stabilization*. This is an important component for limiting injuries in this part of the body. This exercise, while focusing on the muscles of the lower back, is also very good for developing scapular stabilization because the rhomboids contract to pinch the shoulder blades together.

Lying Superman

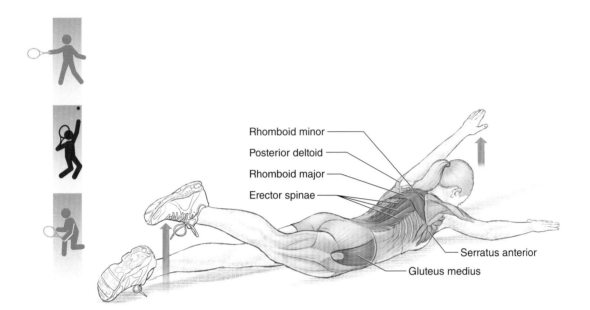

Rhomboid minor
Posterior deltoid
Rhomboid major
Erector spinae
Serratus anterior
Gluteus medius

Execution

1. Lie facedown on the floor, with both arms out straight above your head. Keep your legs straight, with feet on the floor.
2. Raise your left arm off the ground while simultaneously raising your right leg off the ground. Contract the muscles in the lower and upper back. Control the motion, focusing on contracting the back muscles.
3. Return to the starting position, and repeat with your right arm and left leg.

Muscles Involved

Primary: Erector spinae, multifidus, rhomboid major, rhomboid minor, gluteus medius

Secondary: Posterior deltoid, serratus anterior, latissimus dorsi

Tennis Focus

Having good balance and control of opposing upper and lower limbs is important since most strokes in tennis require cross-body movements. A right-handed player's serve requires vigorous involvement from the right side of the upper body, while the left side of the lower body is dominant from a strength and stability standpoint. This requires the lower back and core to be trained in a functional cross-body way.

VARIATION

Flying Superman

The flying Superman version is performed in a similar manner, but you lift both legs and arms at the same time. This makes the exercise more difficult because you have to really maintain control of your back and abdominals. An easier option is the kneeling Superman. Kneel on all fours. As you lift the left arm and right leg, keep the opposing leg and arm on the ground to maintain balance. This exercise works similar muscles but results in less activation of the lower back muscles and more activation of the transversus abdominis and hip stabilizers.

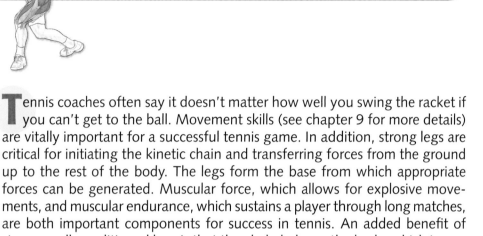

Tennis coaches often say it doesn't matter how well you swing the racket if you can't get to the ball. Movement skills (see chapter 9 for more details) are vitally important for a successful tennis game. In addition, strong legs are critical for initiating the kinetic chain and transferring forces from the ground up to the rest of the body. The legs form the base from which appropriate forces can be generated. Muscular force, which allows for explosive movements, and muscular endurance, which sustains a player through long matches, are both important components for success in tennis. An added benefit of strong, well-conditioned legs is that they help balance the body, which is particularly important when a player is out of position. Strong legs help a player overcome inertia when changing directions, which happens on average four or five times during each point. Each of the tennis strokes is influenced by well-conditioned legs.

Leg Anatomy

The pelvic bones form a ring that connects the spine to the lower limbs. Many of the strongest muscles in the body are connected to the pelvic bones. This allows the weight of the body to be transferred to the legs with great stability. The major bone of the upper leg is the femur, which connects the hip joint to the knee joint. The two major bones of the lower leg are the tibia and the fibula, which connect the knee joint to the ankle joint. The knee joint is a hinge joint and is able to flex and extend, similar to the elbow joint.

The quadriceps, the primary muscle group on the front of the upper leg, is responsible for extending the lower leg. The quadriceps is made up of the rectus femoris, vastus lateralis, vastus medialis, and vastus intermedius (figure 7.1, page 120).

The major gluteal muscles include the gluteus maximus, gluteus medius, and gluteus minimus (figure 7.2, page 120). The gluteus maximus is mainly responsible for extending (straightening) the leg, while the gluteus medius and gluteus minimus work together to hold the pelvis level when you walk or run on the non-weight-bearing leg. The hamstring muscles at the back of the upper leg allow the knee to flex. These muscles include the biceps femoris, semimembranosus, and semitendinosus. Other major upper leg muscles include the gracilis, which assists in flexing the leg, medially rotating the hip, and adducting the thigh; and the sartorius, a long muscle that assists in flexing the thigh as well as extending the knee.

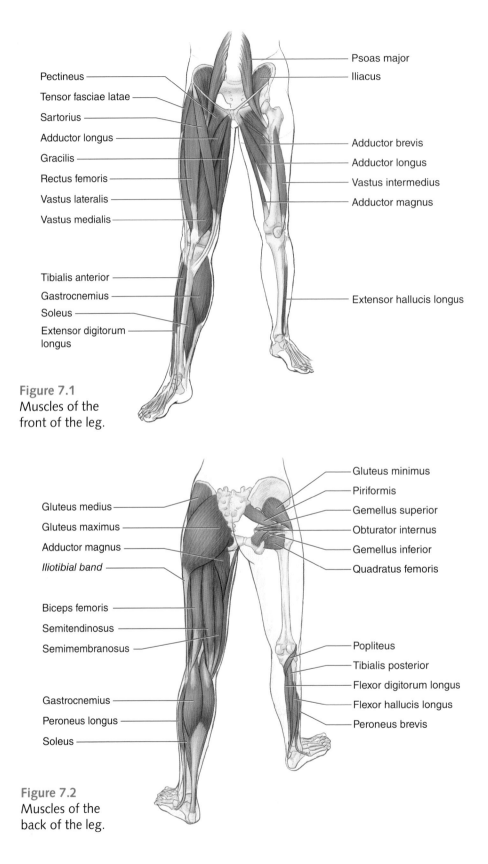

Pectineus

Tensor fasciae latae

Sartorius

Adductor longus

Gracilis

Rectus femoris

Vastus lateralis

Vastus medialis

Tibialis anterior

Gastrocnemius

Soleus

Extensor digitorum
longus

Psoas major

Iliacus

Adductor brevis

Adductor longus

Vastus intermedius

Adductor magnus

Extensor hallucis longus

Figure 7.1
Muscles of the
front of the leg.

Gluteus medius

Gluteus maximus

Adductor magnus

Iliotibial band

Biceps femoris

Semitendinosus

Semimembranosus

Gastrocnemius

Peroneus longus

Soleus

Gluteus minimus

Piriformis

Gemellus superior

Obturator internus

Gemellus inferior

Quadratus femoris

Popliteus

Tibialis posterior

Flexor digitorum longus

Flexor hallucis longus

Peroneus brevis

Figure 7.2
Muscles of the
back of the leg.

120

Three muscle groups make up the muscles of the lower leg. On the posterior side of the lower leg (figure 7.3a), the gastrocnemius and soleus make up the calf muscle. They are responsible for plantar flexion of the foot, which is necessary for a good push-off when running. The anterior muscles of the lower leg (figure 7.3b) include the tibialis anterior, extensor digitorum

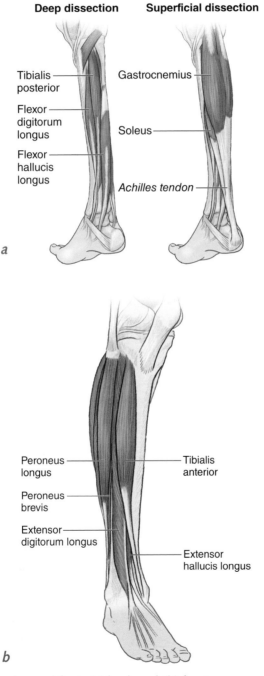

Figure 7.3 Lower leg and foot: *(a)* back and *(b)* front.

longus, and extensor hallucis longus. These muscles are all dorsiflexors of the foot. This means that when they contract, they bring the toes up toward the shin. The lateral muscles of the lower leg are alongside the fibula, the smaller of the two lower leg bones. They include the peroneus longus and the peroneus brevis. Their main objective is to resist the movement of inversion (the sole facing inward). In other words, they help support the ankle by preventing the most common ankle sprain. In addition, they assist with plantar flexion and eversion (the sole facing outward). One other muscle, the popliteus muscle (see figure 7.2 on page 120), is very important to tennis players. It unlocks the knee joint by rotating it slightly to allow the straightened leg to flex. It is one of the deep calf muscles and lies at the back of the knee. Each of these muscles plays an important role when you run, stop, and change directions.

Tennis Strokes and Leg Movement

For good tennis, the legs must provide a strong, stable base of support. Groundstrokes and volleys both start with a split step, during which the muscles of the legs absorb the shock of touching down on the ground, typically followed by an explosive movement in one direction or the other. When a player is pulled wide for a shot, he must recover toward the center of the court. If his legs are well trained and strong, he can recover more quickly and more often without fatigue. Clearly, explosive strength from the legs is useful, but to be able to complete these actions, muscular endurance is also vitally important.

The legs also play an important role in allowing players to repeatedly bend down for low shots. Low volleys, which are often hit in doubles, are a good example of the need for leg strength in these positions.

The serve is the only shot that starts from a stationary position. The legs provide a vertical push-off by flexing and extending forcefully. This action is repeated frequently in a singles match since players serve every other game. The exercises described in this chapter provide foundational strength by training the legs for tennis.

Exercises for the Legs

Box jumps and depth jumps are great plyometric drills that focus on power development, but they are advanced drills. Incorporate them into your training program only after you establish an appropriate strength base for the leg muscles. Tennis requires a lot of running in many directions during play. Therefore, be cautious when introducing more stress by using exercises that require you to land on hard surfaces. Include at least one full day of recovery between leg training sessions. The number of sets and repetitions as well as the resistance used can vary significantly based on many factors such as your base fitness and strength level, your playing schedule, the point in the season, and your performance goals (e.g., power, strength, endurance). Consult a knowledgeable strength and conditioning professional who knows tennis to find out what program might be best for you. This person should also be able to evaluate your posture and technique for each exercise. It is especially easy to overtrain the legs since these muscles are already so active during play.

Squat

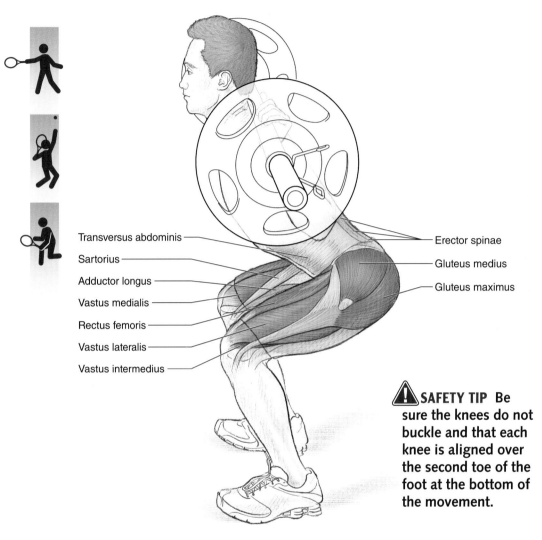

Transversus abdominis

Sartorius

Adductor longus

Vastus medialis

Rectus femoris

Vastus lateralis

Vastus intermedius

Erector spinae

Gluteus medius

Gluteus maximus

⚠ SAFETY TIP Be sure the knees do not buckle and that each knee is aligned over the second toe of the foot at the bottom of the movement.

Execution

1. Place a barbell behind the head and across the shoulders, on top of the trapezius muscle. Hold the bar with the hands at a comfortable width apart, palms facing forward. Squeeze your shoulder blades together. Keep the feet approximately shoulder-width apart, with the toes pointed straight ahead or slightly out.

2. From the starting position, slowly bend the knees and push your weight into your heels. Keep the back straight. Lower your body until your thighs are parallel to the floor.

3. Extend the knees to return to the starting position.

Muscles Involved

Primary: Gluteus maximus, gluteus medius, vastus lateralis, rectus femoris, vastus medialis, vastus intermedius

Secondary: Sartorius, gracilis, adductor longus, adductor brevis, adductor magnus, erector spinae, multifidus, transversus abdominis

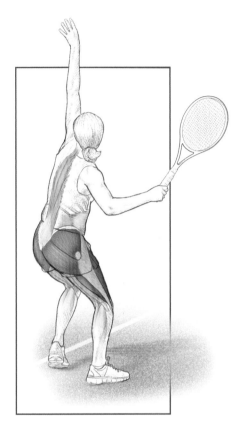

Tennis Focus

The muscles involved in the squat are critical in each of the strokes. These are mostly big, strong muscles that help with the push-off and landing phases in running, changes of direction, and balance and stability in the ready position. Each tennis stroke requires a ready position similar to a squat. Since the serve is typically the hardest stroke hit, it requires a strong, stable base of support. The muscles trained by the squat, both the gluteal muscles and the leg muscles, provide that stable base and allow a player to transfer forces from the ground up to the muscles of the trunk and shoulders.

VARIATION

Front Squat

A variation of the regular squat is the front squat. For the front squat, the barbell is positioned across the anterior deltoids, with your arms crossed and palms across the top of the bar. The front squat focuses primarily on the quadriceps. The key is to keep the back straight to help you stay balanced. Typically, you want to use slightly lighter weights for the front squat.

Romanian Deadlift

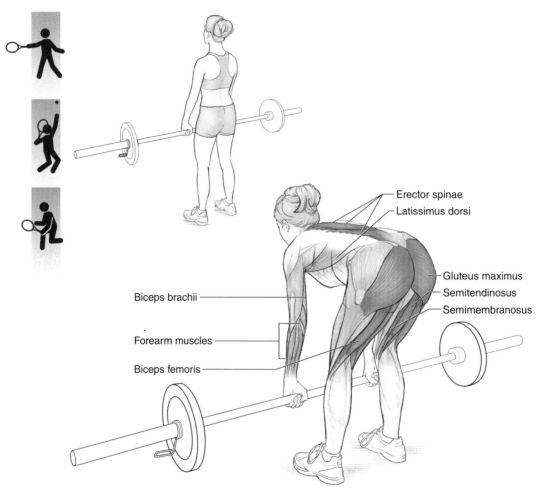

Erector spinae
Latissimus dorsi
Gluteus maximus
Semitendinosus
Semimembranosus
Biceps brachii
Forearm muscles
Biceps femoris

Execution

1. Stand with your feet shoulder-width apart and knees slightly bent (athletic position). Hold a barbell in front of your body, arms down in front of your thighs. The hands are approximately shoulder-width apart, with the palms turned toward the body.

2. Slowly lower the weight to the middle of the shins by hinging at the hips. Your gluteals should go back and up as you maintain a slight anterior pelvic tilt.

3. Lift the weight back up by extending the hips and waist until you are upright, shoulders back.

Muscles Involved

Primary: Biceps femoris, semitendinosus, semimembranosus, gluteus maximus, erector spinae

Secondary: Biceps brachii, latissimus dorsi, forearm muscles

Tennis Focus

Although this exercise benefits all tennis strokes, it is particularly useful for improving forehand and backhand groundstrokes. The Romanian deadlift not only helps strengthen the muscles of the lower back and hamstrings but also improves their flexibility. This exercise is particularly useful in preparing for low forehands and backhands as well as those groundstrokes that require a significant reach. The Romanian deadlift has the dual benefit of improving performance and preventing injury to the muscles and surrounding joints of the hips and knees. This exercise

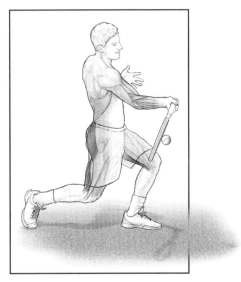

develops eccentric strength in the hip extensor muscles, which are vitally important during landing and change-of-direction movements on the court.

Hamstring Buck

Soleus

Gastrocnemius

Semimembranosus

Semitendinosus

Biceps femoris

Gluteus maximus

Gluteus medius

Execution

1. Lie on your back, with your left knee bent at approximately 45 degrees and your left heel pressing into the floor so that your left toe points to the ceiling. Your right leg is extended straight in the air, with your right toe pointing to the ceiling.

2. Raise your hips and lower back off the floor by pushing your weight into your left heel. Hold this position at the top for two seconds, and then lower to the starting position.

3. After performing one set on the left leg, switch legs and repeat the movement using your right leg.

Muscles Involved

Primary: Biceps femoris, popliteus, semitendinosus, semimembranosus, gluteus maximus, gluteus medius

Secondary: Gastrocnemius, soleus

Tennis Focus

Developing hamstring and hip extensor strength and stability is very important in all tennis movements that require lower body deceleration. Stopping and changing direction happen often during a single tennis match. The stronger your hamstring and hip extension strength, the more force you can handle. This allows you to stop faster and change direction quicker. Hamstring and gluteal eccentric strength are needed when landing on open-stance groundstrokes and especially when hitting low volleys that require great stability at contact. Closed-stance backhand volleys are a great example of when the hamstrings and gluteals are activated eccentrically to successfully execute the stroke.

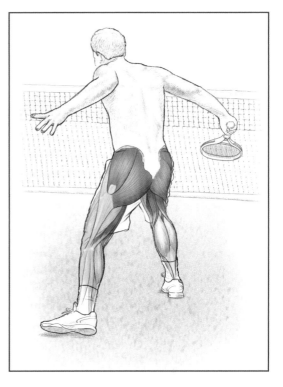

VARIATION

Exercise Ball Hamstring Buck

The hamstring buck can be adapted through a series of progressions to make the movement more challenging. Once you are able to perform the hamstring buck on the floor comfortably, progress as appropriate by placing your heel on more challenging, less stable surfaces. For example, for the exercise ball variation, the foot is on an exercise ball, and the knee is bent about 90 degrees. Progress from the floor to a bench to a BOSU ball to the exercise ball to a medicine ball to a tennis ball and finally to a golf ball. The last few variations in the progression are very challenging.

Linear Lunge

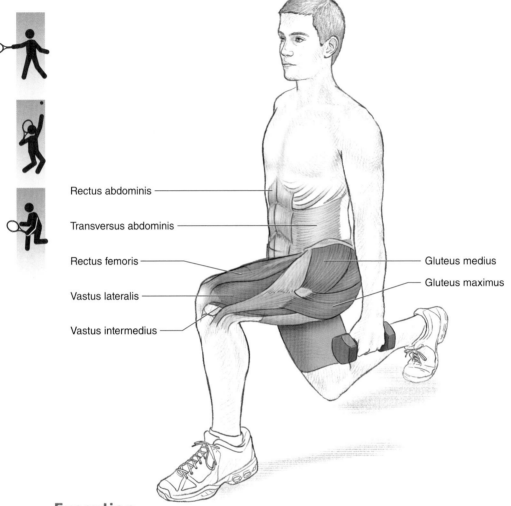

Rectus abdominis

Transversus abdominis

Rectus femoris

Vastus lateralis

Vastus intermedius

Gluteus medius

Gluteus maximus

Execution

1. Stand with your feet shoulder-width apart. Hold a dumbbell in each hand. Arms are straight at the sides, palms turned toward the body. Keep your shoulders back and down, your head up, and your core stable.

2. Keeping an upright posture, step forward with one foot, absorbing the load of the body and flexing the front knee 90 degrees into a lunge position. The thigh is parallel to the floor. Make sure the knee bends no more than 90 degrees. The hips and shoulders remain square. The trail leg stays as straight as possible without the back knee touching the floor.

3. Immediately push off the front foot, and return to the starting position. Repeat, stepping forward with the other foot. Alternate right and left.

Muscles Involved

Primary: Gluteus maximus, gluteus medius, rectus femoris, vastus intermedius, vastus lateralis

Secondary: Rectus abdominis, transversus abdominis

Tennis Focus

Lunges are particularly tennis-specific to volleys. Although the focus in a volley is often on the hands, the legs get the player in the proper position so the upper body can be balanced for the stroke. The movement pattern of the linear lunge mimics the position the body is in for both forehand and backhand volleys. Proper technique while executing the linear lunge will help with the technical aspect of the volley as well. Both the linear lunge and the volley require good balance, control over the center of gravity, and proper posture.

VARIATION

Linear Lunge With Medicine Ball

Lunge while holding a medicine ball behind the head and neck. This changes the balance slightly by raising your center of mass. In tennis, a player has to control her center of gravity and balance in a variety of positions. This variation of the linear lunge not only focuses the player on proper balance with a raised center of gravity but also requires the player to strengthen the core to be able to hold this position. Both benefits help players perform each stroke in a more controlled manner. Focus on keeping the head and chest up.

Lateral Lunge

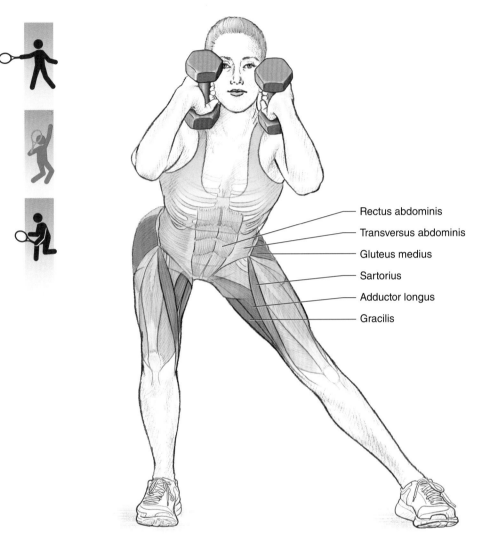

Rectus abdominis

Transversus abdominis

Gluteus medius

Sartorius

Adductor longus

Gracilis

Execution

1. Stand with your feet shoulder-width apart and a dumbbell in each hand. Rest the dumbbells on your shoulders, with the elbows pointed forward.

2. Keeping an upright posture, step to the side with one foot, absorbing the load of the body and flexing the knee until the thigh is almost parallel to the floor. The trail leg will be slightly bent, with the toes pointing straight ahead.

3. Push off and return to the starting position. Switch legs and repeat the movement to the other side. Alternate right and left.

Muscles Involved

Primary: Adductor longus, adductor brevis, gluteus medius, gracilis, sartorius

Secondary: Rectus abdominis, transversus abdominis, erector spinae

Tennis Focus

In essence, the lateral lunge is a variation of the regular (linear) lunge. However, the focus in the lateral lunge is to mimic or replicate the movement pattern of a wide volley. In a wide volley, most of the body weight is distributed on the leg closest to the oncoming ball. The lateral lunge produces a similar motion. To avoid additional stress on the joints, execute the lunge with the feet pointing forward. Both abductors (eccentrically) and adductors (concentrically) will be very active during this movement. These muscle groups are crucial in the recovery phase between shots.

45-Degree Lunge

Transversus abdominis

Gluteus medius

Rectus femoris

Gluteus maximus

Vastus intermedius

Execution

1. Stand with your feet shoulder-width apart and a dumbbell in each hand. Arms are at the sides, with the palms turned toward the body.

2. Keeping an upright posture, step at a 45-degree angle with one foot, absorbing the load of the body and flexing at the knee until the thigh is almost parallel to the floor. The trail leg will be bent.

3. Push off and return to the starting position. Switch legs, stepping at a 45-degree angle with the other foot. Alternate right and left.

Muscles Involved

Primary: Rectus femoris, gluteus maximus, vastus intermedius

Secondary: Gluteus medius, transversus abdominis

Tennis Focus

The 45-degree angle of this lunge most closely resembles the proper technique of a volley in tennis. The advantage of executing the lunge at a 45-degree angle is that it teaches the player to focus on closing in on the net at an angle when hitting a volley. This allows the player to transfer the body weight forward while making contact. As in the volley, this lunge should be performed with proper technique. Focus on bending at the knees, not the back. The hips, knees, and ankles should remain aligned for proper balance.

Crossover Lunge

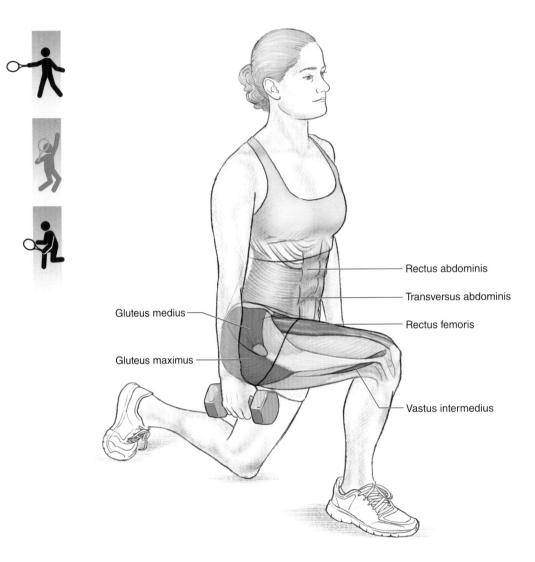

Rectus abdominis

Transversus abdominis

Rectus femoris

Gluteus medius

Gluteus maximus

Vastus intermedius

Execution

1. Stand with your feet shoulder-width apart and a dumbbell in each hand. Arms are at the sides, with the palms turned toward the body.

2. Keeping an upright posture, cross one foot over the other at a 45-degree angle and lunge, absorbing the load of the body and flexing at the knee until the thigh is almost parallel to the floor. The trail leg will be bent.

3. Push off and return to the starting position. Switch legs, stepping over with the other foot. Alternate right and left.

Muscles Involved

Primary: Rectus femoris, gluteus maximus, gluteus medius, gluteus minimus, vastus intermedius

Secondary: Rectus abdominis, transversus abdominis

Tennis Focus

Although the modern game features frequent strokes hit with open stances, sometimes a closed stance is needed. Therefore, the body has to be properly prepared for this particular stroke. The crossover lunge is similar to a closed-stance groundstroke. Specifically, it most closely resembles the movement used in a one-handed backhand. When executing this particular lunge, point the toes to the sides when stepping out so that the hips, knees, and ankles remain properly aligned.

Box Jump

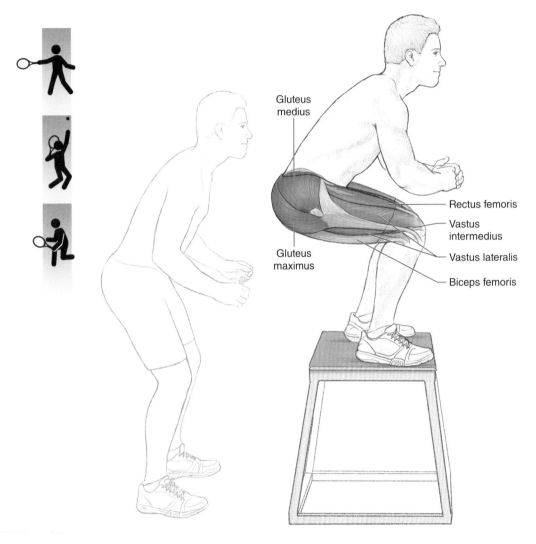

Gluteus
medius

Rectus femoris

Vastus
intermedius

Gluteus
maximus

Vastus lateralis

Biceps femoris

Execution

1. You will need a 12- to 42-inch (30 to 107 cm) box, depending on your ability. Stand facing the box, approximately 1 to 2 feet (.3 to .6 m) from it, with feet shoulder-width apart.

2. Jump up onto the box. Focus on touching down as softly as possible on top of the box and sitting back into your hips. This develops good landing mechanics and reduces the impact on the knee joints.

3. Jump off the box, back to the starting position. Focus on absorbing the shock and landing as softly as possible. Keep your chest upright, and maintain a solid posture to absorb the forces produced during the landing.

Muscles Involved

Primary: Gluteus maximus, gluteus medius, rectus femoris, vastus lateralis, vastus medialis, vastus intermedius

Secondary: Biceps femoris, semitendinosus, semimembranosus

Tennis Focus

This is an excellent plyometric drill. The focus is on training the legs for explosive movements, which are required quite often during the course of a match such as when changing direction. In addition, training the legs for explosive power helps develop a better tennis serve. The legs play an important role in transferring force from the ground up to the rest of the body. Strong legs also permit proper knee flexion and extension in the loading phase of the serve.

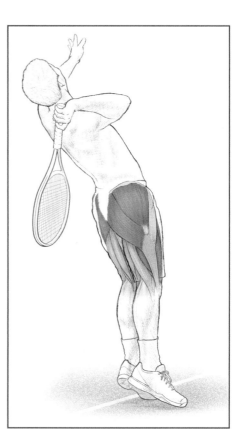

VARIATION

Single-Leg Box Jump

A more advanced version of the box jump, in which you jump with both legs, is the single-leg box jump, in which you jump with only one leg. This jump requires a considerable amount of strength and coordination and is a highly advanced exercise. It is recommended only for advanced players. The single-leg box jump may be performed with either leg. Use a box that is lower than the box used for the regular box jump—one that is 4 to 16 inches (10 to 40 cm) high.

Depth Jump

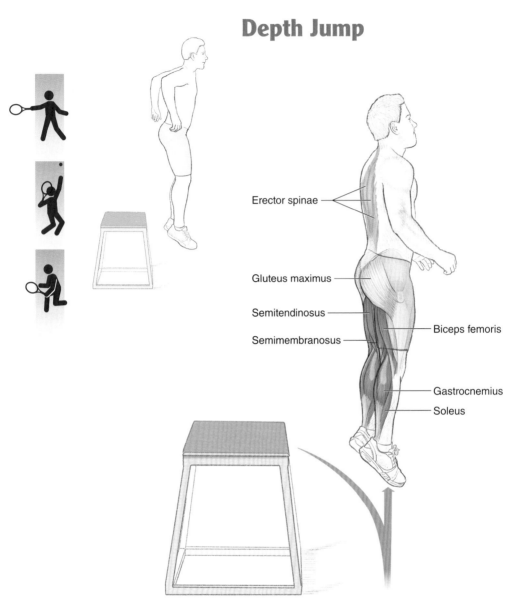

Erector spinae

Gluteus maximus

Semitendinosus

Semimembranosus

Biceps femoris

Gastrocnemius

Soleus

Execution

1. You will need a 12- to 24-inch (30 to 60 cm) box, depending on your ability. Stand on top of the box.

2. Step down from the box, landing on both feet. Immediately after landing, spring up. Try to touch down on the ground for as short a time as possible.

3. When you spring up, you can simply jump straight up, or you can jump on top of another box to repeat the sequence.

Muscles Involved

Primary: Rectus abdominis, biceps femoris, semitendinosus, semimembranosus, gastrocnemius, soleus

Secondary: Erector spinae, gluteus maximus

Tennis Focus

The depth jump is another excellent plyometric exercise for improving both the strength and speed components of the leg muscles. The depth jump is a highly tennis-specific way of training. Movement skills in all directions and the strength needed for a powerful serve can be trained this way. Depth jumps help players shorten the time on the ground during movements on the tennis court, allowing players to move and change directions quickly. Another great benefit of the depth jump is that the leg muscles used during the serve are trained very specifically.

VARIATION

Depth Jump Into Hurdle Hop

After landing from the depth jump, continue to jump over a series of mini hurdles set up in a straight line from the box. Focus on keeping the hips and shoulders square, and continue to touch down on the ground for as short a time as possible.

Calf Raise

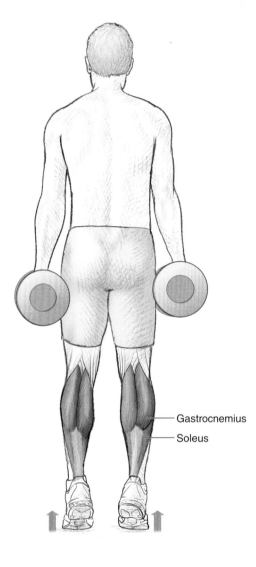

Gastrocnemius
Soleus

Execution

1. Stand with your feet shoulder-width apart, and hold a dumbbell in each hand. Arms are at your sides, with the palms turned toward the body.

2. Rise on your toes as high as possible while maintaining good balance. The only joint action should be at the ankle joint.

3. Hold for one to two seconds, and then slowly lower to the starting position.

Muscles Involved

Primary: Gastrocnemius, soleus

Tennis Focus

The job of the calf muscles is to plantar flex the foot. This very important movement permits the strong push-off action necessary for running and jumping. Specifically, the gastrocnemius, a large muscle with mostly vertical fibers, provides this push-off action. The calf muscles allow the heels to be lifted against the whole body weight. Therefore, they play a major role in each tennis stroke. A great example of the importance of the calf muscles can be seen in the serve. In the loading phase, when the forces from the ground are being transferred to the rest of the body, the gastrocnemius and soleus go into action. Because of this forceful action, many players actually come off the ground when serving.

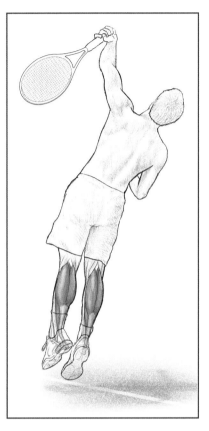

VARIATION

Advanced Calf Raise

To make this exercise more difficult, increase the range of motion. Stand on a block or the edge of a machine so the heels hang lower than the balls of the feet. Rise up onto the toes.

CHAPTER 8 ROTATIONAL STRENGTHENING

The modern tennis game has changed significantly over the past 30 years. New training techniques and in particular new racket technology have led to changes in the way the ball is struck. Specifically, the forehand and backhand groundstrokes have benefited from these changes. The new rackets are made of different materials, typically composite materials instead of wood or metal, and have larger racket heads. This makes them stiffer, stronger, lighter, and slightly more forgiving on mis-hits. This technology allows players to have swing patterns that are more rotational in nature. In sync with the development of this equipment, training techniques both on and off the court have changed, putting a greater emphasis on strengthening the muscle groups responsible for the rotational component of each stroke.

Anatomy of Rotation

A solid base is required for effective rotational movements in tennis. Therefore strengthening the legs, especially through multijoint exercises, is critical. The gluteus maximus and quadriceps muscles absorb the shock when you land or change direction. They also help create explosive action when you push off to run and provide a solid base when you hit a groundstroke from an open stance. Similarly, the gastrocnemius and soleus muscles in the lower leg must be strong during these shots.

Strengthening the core, or midsection, should receive a great deal of emphasis as well. The internal and external obliques are very critical for rotational movement in tennis strokes, but the transversus abdominis, multifidus, erector spinae, iliacus, and psoas major also provide strength and muscular balance during rotation.

Because tennis strokes have become more forceful, it has become necessary to emphasize the musculature of the upper body as well. Muscles such as the latissimus dorsi, serratus anterior, trapezius, rhomboids, and levator scapulae all play important roles in protecting the shoulder joint and scapular region during each stroke. They work in concert to help with the actual swing as well as to provide stability.

Tennis Strokes and Rotation

Tennis requires multijoint movements. Forces are transferred from the lower body to the upper body through a sequence of muscle actions. In the modern game, the rotational component of the swing has become more important. Groundstrokes in particular feature open-stance and semi-open-stance strokes more than ever. Forehands and two-handed backhands are commonly hit with a tremendous amount of rotation. Therefore the legs need to provide a solid platform to push off against. Exercises to strengthen the legs are vital to prepare the body for forceful shots.

The torso and midsection provide the greatest amount of rotational force; therefore, very specific exercises are required to prepare the body. The more tennis-specific the exercise, the better. You want to overload the same muscles used during the strokes by using the same or similar movement patterns as those used during each stroke. Although you should try to mimic the movement patterns of the strokes, muscles that function eccentrically in the follow-through of strokes are typically trained in a concentric manner as well, especially early on in a training program when the focus should be on establishing a baseline strength level. As you get stronger, add the eccentric component of training. This will maintain an appropriate strength balance between anterior and posterior movement patterns such as the backswing and follow-through. If a muscle imbalance becomes too large, it could result in greater risk of injury. Balanced training helps protect the joints. This concept applies to the muscles of the upper body as well since vigorous rotations require significant strength in the rotator cuff and scapular region. Although mostly highlighted in the groundstrokes, rotation plays a role in every stroke. The exercises in this chapter are critical for both performance enhancement and injury prevention.

Exercises for Rotational Strength

The following exercises that develop rotational strength are highly tennis specific. They are multijoint, multiplane exercises that involve the whole body. Many of them mimic actual stroke patterns. In addition to developing strength, these exercises improve flexibility because most require a full range of motion. Focus on proper technique throughout each of the movement patterns. Each exercise can be performed with more or less weight, depending on your strength, and more or less speed, depending on your training goal. Work with a qualified strength and conditioning coach with a good knowledge of tennis when performing these exercises to make sure you perform them properly. Start with two or three sets of 10 to 12 repetitions. The amount of resistance used, the number of repetitions performed, and the number of sets performed will change based on your goals, strengths and weaknesses, requirements for rest and recovery, and playing schedule in a structured periodized training program.

Cable Rotational Chop

Latissimus dorsi
Serratus anterior
External oblique
Internal oblique
Transversus abdominis

Execution

1. Set a cable pulley machine in a high starting position (shoulder height or slightly higher). Stand with your left side next to the machine. Tighten your core, and pull your shoulders back.

2. Grab the cable pulley handle with both hands, and pull diagonally across your body with straight arms from high to low, left shoulder to right hip. Isolate the upper body action. This movement strengthens the muscles related to the serve and forehand for a left-handed player.

3. Perform the appropriate repetitions, and then repeat the same procedure on the other side, moving from the right shoulder to the left hip. This movement strengthens the muscles related to the backhand for a left-handed player.

Muscles Involved

Primary: Latissimus dorsi (backhand motion), internal oblique, external oblique, transversus abdominis

Secondary: Serratus anterior, erector spinae

Tennis Focus

Since the modern tennis game is dominated by serves and forehands, training the muscle groups conducive to success in these strokes is vital. The cable rotational chop and the cable rotational lift (page 150) in particular help train the muscles that assist in the forward action of both the serve and forehand when performed on the dominant side of the body. The primary muscles work concentrically (shorten) to provide the force in the forward swing, while the secondary muscles act eccentrically (lengthen) to help maintain balance, provide stability, and support the body. When performed on the nondominant side of the body, this exercise mimics and benefits the backhand. The nature of this multijoint exercise is similar to hitting high forehands and backhands.

VARIATION

Cable Rotational Chop With Hip Rotation

In this variation, the upper body follows the same movement pattern as in the primary exercise, but in addition the hips rotate at the same time as the upper body. This movement more closely mimics the actual movement in a tennis stroke and allows for a greater range of motion.

For a more advanced version of the cable rotational chop, use a lighter resistance and only one hand.

Cable Rotational Lift

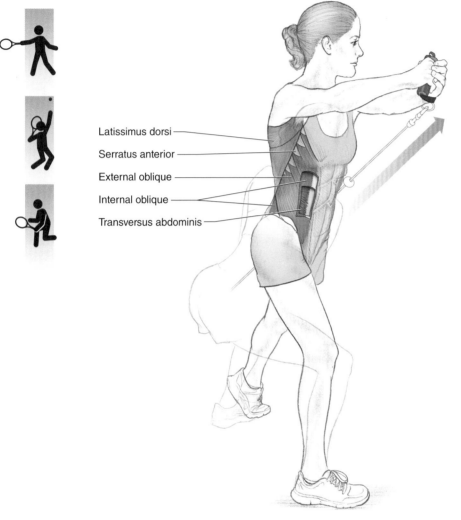

Latissimus dorsi

Serratus anterior

External oblique

Internal oblique

Transversus abdominis

Execution

1. Set a cable pulley machine in a low starting position (hip height or slightly lower). Stand with your left side next to the machine. Tighten your core, and pull your shoulders back and down.

2. Grab the cable pulley handle with both hands, and pull diagonally across the body with straight arms from low to high, left hip to right shoulder. Isolate the upper body action. This movement strengthens the muscles related to the backhand for a right-handed player.

3. Perform the appropriate number of repetitions, and then repeat the same procedure on the other side, moving from the right hip to the left shoulder. This movement strengthens the muscles related to the serve and forehand for a right-handed player.

Muscles Involved

Primary: Latissimus dorsi (backhand motion), internal oblique, external oblique, transversus abdominis

Secondary: Serratus anterior, erector spinae

Tennis Focus

The cable rotational lift and cable rotational chop (page 148), when performed on the nondominant side of the body, involve the same muscle groups a right-handed player uses in the backhand stroke. Specifically, in the movement pattern from low to high, the exercise follows a similar path as the topspin backhand. An additional benefit of this exercise is that some of the primary muscles that act concentrically during the backhand and the exercise also act eccentrically during the serve and forehand. The concentric nature of this exercise helps strengthen these muscles, thereby protecting them from injury in addition to improving performance. When performed on the dominant side of the body, the cable rotational lift benefits the muscles a right-handed player uses in the forehand stroke.

VARIATION

Cable Rotational Lift With Hip Rotation

The upper body follows the same movement pattern as in the cable rotational lift, but in addition the hips rotate at the same time as the upper body. This movement more closely mimics the actual muscles involved in the tennis stroke and allows for a greater range of motion.

Single-Arm Rotational Dumbbell Snatch

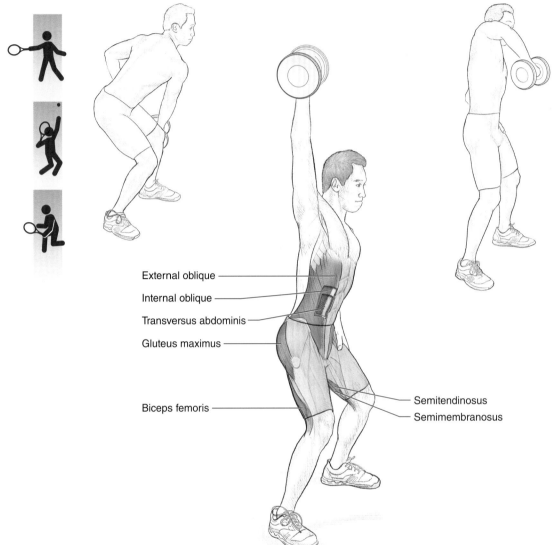

External oblique

Internal oblique

Transversus abdominis

Gluteus maximus

Biceps femoris

Semitendinosus

Semimembranosus

Execution

1. If you are a right-handed player, stand with a dumbbell in your right hand. (A left-handed player holds a dumbbell in the left hand.) Hold your right hand diagonally across your body, slightly outside your left knee. Maintain a tight and stable core and a slight bend in your knees, with feet about shoulder-width apart.

2. Rapidly move the dumbbell diagonally from the left knee or hip to an overhead position to the right of the head, ending with the arm extended beside the head. Keep the elbow straight.

3. Perform the appropriate number of repetitions, and then repeat with the opposite arm for coordination and muscular balance.

Muscles Involved

Primary: Gluteus maximus, biceps femoris, semitendinosus, semimembranosus, iliacus, psoas major, transversus abdominis, internal oblique, external oblique

Secondary: Erector spinae, multifidus

Tennis Focus

This particular exercise involves the same muscle groups used in the backhand stroke. Specifically, in the movement pattern from low to high, the exercise follows a path similar to the topspin backhand. An additional benefit of this exercise is that some of the primary muscles that act concentrically during the backhand and this exercise also act eccentrically during the serve and forehand. The concentric nature of these exercises helps strengthen these muscles, thereby protecting them from injury and improving performance. Because this is a free-weight exercise, additional stabilizing muscles are called into play to balance the body. These stabilizing muscles are also active during the backhand stroke. When performed correctly, this explosive exercise focused on the lower body and core helps develop power that can be directly transferred to all tennis strokes.

VARIATION

Single-Arm Rotational Dumbbell Snatch With Hip Rotation

The starting position is the same as for the single-arm rotational dumbbell snatch. The upper body follows the same movement pattern as in the single-arm rotational dumbbell snatch, but in addition the hips rotate at the same time as the dumbbell. Because of the explosiveness of the movement, the feet may come off the ground. This movement more closely mimics the actual movement involved in the tennis stroke and allows for a greater range of motion.

Dumbbell Jump Shrug

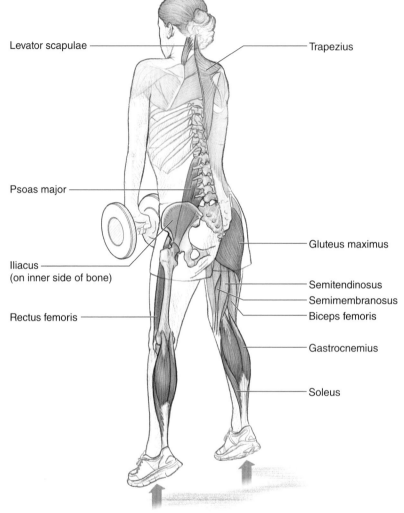

Levator scapulae

Trapezius

Psoas major

Gluteus maximus

Iliacus
(on inner side of bone)

Semitendinosus

Semimembranosus

Rectus femoris

Biceps femoris

Gastrocnemius

Soleus

Execution

1. Stand with your feet shoulder-width apart. Tilting slightly forward at the waist, keep your shoulders back, core tight and stable, and head relaxed with eyes looking forward. Hold a relatively light dumbbell in each hand in front of your body, with your arms hanging straight down. Dumbbells are just above knee level. Knees are flexed in an athletic position.

2. Explosively jump up by extending the ankles, knees, and hips. Jump as high as you can while simultaneously shrugging the shoulders.

3. Land softly with your feet shoulder-width apart. Slightly bend the knees to avoid excessive loading at the knees, hips, and lower back.

Muscles Involved

Primary: Gluteus maximus, rectus femoris, iliacus, psoas major, gastrocnemius, soleus

Secondary: Trapezius, levator scapulae, biceps femoris, semitendinosus, semimembranosus

Tennis Focus

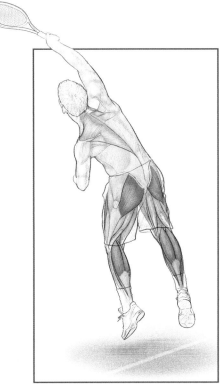

This is a great exercise to strengthen the muscles used in the serve and overhead. Although the trunk moves in flexion and extension, this exercise uses the same muscles that provide key stabilization and rotation. The knee flexion and extension mimic the explosive component of the upward drive of the legs when you serve or hit an overhead. Overloading the body by using weights helps strengthen the legs to provide a forceful action and also to assist with muscular endurance. Because this exercise is focused on power development, use a relatively light weight, approximately 30 to 50 percent of your one-repetition maximum (1RM) (see chapter 1, page 19).

VARIATION

Barbell Jump Shrug

Use a barbell instead of dumbbells. It may be easier to use a barbell since the dumbbells require more stabilization throughout the body during the exercise for you to control them during the jump.

Overhead Squat

Posterior deltoid
Rhomboid minor
Rhomboid major
Erector spinae
Gluteus maximus
Transversus abdominis
Rectus femoris
Gastrocnemius
Soleus

Execution

1. Press a light barbell from a position behind or in front of the head to an overhead position. The arms should form a 45-degree angle to the bar, and the legs should be approximately shoulder-width apart. Tighten your core, and keep it stable. Squeeze your shoulder blades together.

2. In a slow, controlled movement, flex the knees so that the upper legs end up parallel to the floor or deeper if your flexibility allows and you can maintain good form. Make sure the knees are lined up behind the toes, the back is flat, the chest is out, and the head is up with the eyes forward.

3. Use the legs to drive back up to the starting position while breathing out. Continue to face forward.

Muscles Involved

Primary: Gluteus maximus, rectus femoris, rhomboid major, rhomboid minor, posterior deltoid, gastrocnemius, soleus

Secondary: Transversus abdominis, erector spinae

Tennis Focus

This is a great full-body exercise that requires balance and stability in the midsection, strength in the arms and shoulders, and strength and power in the legs. It is also a very good exercise to improve flexibility in the hips, lower back, and upper back and shoulders. This exercise is particularly beneficial for improving the serve. The knee flexion and extension motion mimics the service action and at the same time overloads the muscles. The trunk has to provide stability during this action, while the isometric hold required to maintain the barbell above the head helps strengthen the muscles of the shoulders.

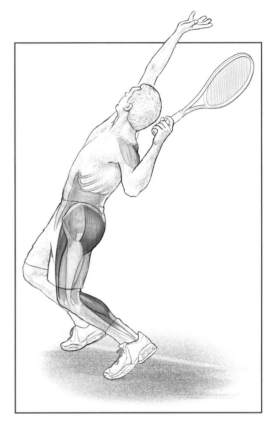

Forehand Medicine Ball Toss

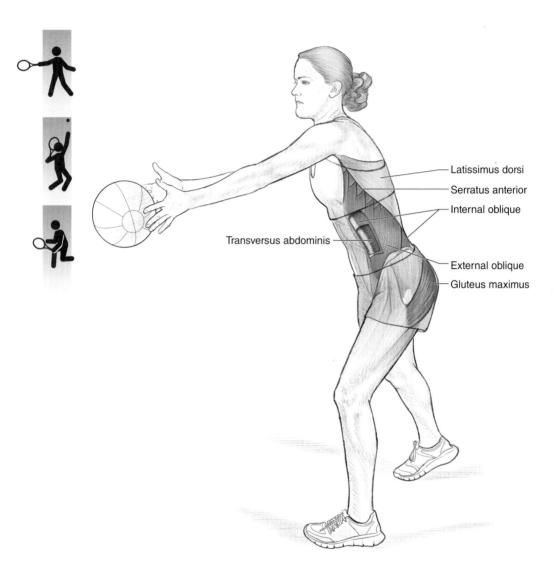

Latissimus dorsi

Serratus anterior

Internal oblique

Transversus abdominis

External oblique

Gluteus maximus

Execution

1. Stand holding a 4- to 6-pound (2 to 3 kg) medicine ball with both hands. Face a partner or a wall approximately 10 feet (3 m) away.

2. Take one step forward so your body is in a side-facing position, and toss the medicine ball to your partner or the wall, mimicking a square-stance forehand stroke.

3. Repeat for 30 seconds.

Muscles Involved

Primary: Serratus anterior, internal oblique, external oblique, transversus abdominis, gluteus maximus

Secondary: Latissimus dorsi, erector spinae

Tennis Focus

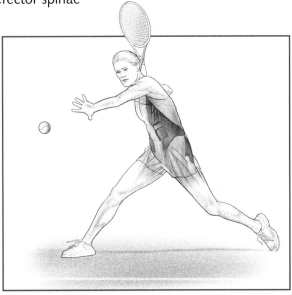

The use of the medicine ball makes strength training very specific to the actual strokes, in this case the forehand stroke. The same muscles activated during the forehand stroke are activated during the forehand medicine ball toss. This training will help provide an explosive stroke while enhancing muscular endurance. Specifically, the rotational muscles of the hips and core—gluteus maximus, obliques, transversus abdominis, and serratus anterior—are developed via a plyometric (stretch–shortening cycle) movement. We recommend performing this movement with both closed and open (see the variation) stances for best results.

VARIATION

Forehand Medicine Ball Toss With Open Stance

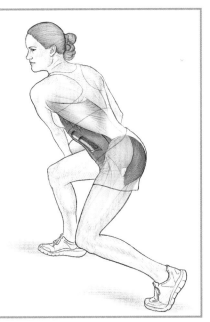

Instead of stepping forward with the left foot (for a right-handed player), stay in the starting position, and complete the toss from a forward-facing stance. This is a more advanced exercise. Because the legs and forward weight transfer do not contribute to the motion, this variation puts more stress on the muscles of the core.

Backhand Medicine Ball Toss

Latissimus dorsi
Serratus anterior
External oblique
Internal oblique
Transversus abdominis

Execution

1. Stand holding a 4- to 6-pound (2 to 3 kg) medicine ball in both hands. Face a partner or a wall approximately 10 feet (3 m) away.

2. Take one step forward so your body is in a side-facing position, and toss the medicine ball, mimicking a backhand stroke.

3. Repeat for 30 seconds.

Muscles Involved

Primary: Latissimus dorsi, internal oblique, external oblique, transversus abdominis, gluteus maximus

Secondary: Serratus anterior, erector spinae

Tennis Focus

The backhand medicine ball toss closely mimics the backhand tennis stroke, particularly the two-handed backhand, and uses the same muscle groups. The use of the medicine ball increases the muscle activity of the trunk, not only by adding resistance but also by making the player focus on stability and balance, key ingredients of a successful backhand. The medicine ball toss uses the muscles of the upper and lower body while focusing on the midsection. This movement helps develop explosive power as well as stability through the core muscles, which translates into more power for your groundstrokes.

VARIATION

Backhand Medicine Ball Toss With Open Stance

Instead of stepping forward with the right foot (for a right-handed player), stay in the starting position, and complete the toss from a forward-facing stance. This is a more advanced exercise. It puts more stress on the muscles of the midsection since the legs and forward weight transfer do not contribute to the movement.

Serve Medicine Ball Toss

Triceps brachii
Serratus anterior
Latissimus dorsi

Transversus abdominis

Gluteus maximus

Execution

1. Stand holding a 4- to 6-pound (2 to 3 kg) medicine ball overhead in both hands. Your feet are shoulder-width apart, and your core is tight and stable. Face a partner or a wall approximately 10 feet (3 m) away.

2. Toss the medicine ball from the overhead position.

3. Repeat for 30 seconds.

Muscles Involved

Primary: Latissimus dorsi, triceps brachii

Secondary: Transversus abdominis, serratus anterior, erector spinae, gluteus maximus

Tennis Focus

This is a great full-body exercise with an emphasis on the core. Even so, this exercise does recruit muscles from the lower body, generating ground reaction forces that move up through the kinetic chain via the core muscles and are finally released through the upper extremities when the medicine ball is released. Because the serve is arguably the most important shot in tennis, the muscles involved in this exercise are vitally important in a comprehensive training program.

VARIATION

Serve Medicine Ball Toss With Open Stance

Instead of keeping the feet shoulder-width apart and grounded, you can perform this exercise with a step forward. Step with the front serving leg (left foot for a right-handed player) to mimic the service motion even more and develop the ability to move forces from the back leg to the front leg. This also adds to the complexity of the movement pattern.

MOVEMENT DRILLS

As all good tennis players know, it doesn't matter how well you can hit the ball if you cannot get to it. Proper movement skills are vitally important for success on the tennis court. Tennis requires movement in all directions. You may have to sprint forward to reach a drop shot, back up for an overhead, or move from side to side to reach wide forehands and backhands. Tennis success comes down to being able to perform short bursts of movement in multiple directions for an extended period of time. All this has to be accomplished while maintaining balance and control over your body and preparing for your shots. The movement drills described in this chapter provide tennis-specific movement patterns in a drill format.

Movement Anatomy

Before any tennis stroke except the serve, you need to be in a good athletic position (figure 9.1, page 166). This position helps you balance and allows you to move quickly in any direction. In an athletic position, you will be on the balls of your feet, with your knees and hips slightly bent and the racket out in front of your body, your elbows bent but relaxed. An athletic position puts your muscles on alert so you can quickly move to where the next ball is hit.

A split step will help you prepare for an athletic position. Perform a split step before each stroke during a rally. A split step is like the unweighting technique skiers use when they turn. When you quickly bend your knees, you take the weight off your feet for a split second. When you land, you can increase the force against the ground, which allows you to push off in any direction.

If you expect a wide ball, typically you will want to slightly turn your feet by using an external hip rotation in the direction of the ball while you are still in the air. Your toes will point in the direction you want to go. This will help you move laterally. The main focus of movement in all directions is on the lower body musculature, with a particular emphasis on the gluteus maximus, gluteus medius, quadriceps, gastrocnemius, and soleus. Lateral and diagonal movements require a greater recruitment of both the abductors and adductors as major contributors in addition to the aforementioned muscles.

Tennis Strokes and Movement

Getting into a proper athletic position helps you with balance and posture and allows you to contract the right muscles to be able to move in any direction. Since the athletic position is necessary to prepare for each of the tennis strokes during a rally, the main focus is on keeping the center of mass between the

Figure 9.1 Athletic position: knees and hips bent slightly, racket in front of body, and elbows bent.

feet, the base of support. The concept of unweighting can help tremendously in the performance of tennis movement skills. By quickly decreasing and increasing your force against the ground, you can acquire balance and then explode to the next shot in any direction as quickly and forcefully as necessary. The most important factor is to be prepared to move in any direction. Overall, you may have to run several miles throughout a match, but being able to sprint, stop, start, and change directions is at least as important. In addition, as you improve you will learn to recognize specific patterns as well as where your opponent is most likely to hit the next shot. This is called anticipation. Being able to anticipate and react quickly to a specific situation on the court will help you get in position early for your next shot, allowing you to take a more balanced and forceful stroke.

Guidelines for Movement Drills

Being able to move well on the court is a huge component of successful tennis. If you can't get there, you can't hit the ball. This oversimplifies the game, but there is a lot of truth to it. We recommend you work on movement skills daily. In fact, many of the drills in this chapter can be performed with racket in hand and can even be incorporated into your on-court hitting sessions. The best way to incorporate movement drills is to make them part of each on-court practice session. They can be added at any time during practice based on your individual needs. In all movement drills, focus on proper balance, fast response time, and quick recovery. Stay light on your feet, and use good technique. If you dedicate a separate training time to movement skills, add an extra 15 to 30 minutes to work on speed and agility at the end of the tennis practice to focus on improving movement skills when you are fatigued.

Lateral Shuffle

Transversus abdominis

Gluteus medius

Tensor fasciae latae

Gluteus medius

Adductor longus

Iliotibial band

Adductor magnus

Gracilis

Execution

1. Start in an athletic position, with your feet shoulder-width apart, knees slightly bent, and eyes forward. Stand at the baseline center mark with the racket in your dominant hand.

2. While maintaining a low, balanced center of mass, perform five shuffles to the left. To perform a shuffle, stay in an athletic position as you bring your feet together and move laterally without crossing the feet.

3. After five shuffles to the left, push off the outside left leg and shuffle back to the baseline center mark.

4. Repeat the movement to the right.

Muscles Involved

Primary: Adductor longus, adductor brevis, adductor magnus, gracilis, gluteus medius, iliotibial band

Secondary: Transversus abdominis, tensor fasciae latae, gluteus maximus, gluteus minimus

Tennis Focus

Lateral movement contributes to 60 to 80 percent of all tennis movements. Therefore, this movement pattern is vital for success on the court. Lateral movement is the main way players get to most groundstrokes, especially neutral balls during rallies. The abductors and adductors along with the gluteus medius help you maintain a low center of mass as you shuffle laterally to get in position to hit well-balanced groundstrokes.

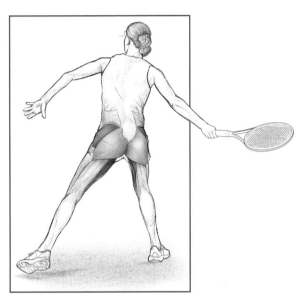

VARIATION

Weighted Lateral Shuffle

The same movement pattern can be performed as you hold a medicine ball in front of the body at hip height. To add difficulty, extend the arms. Another variation includes wearing a weighted vest as you perform the movement. This increases the force required to perform the movement pattern.

Lateral Shuffle With Crossover

Transversus abdominis
Gluteus medius
Gluteus maximus
Tensor fasciae latae
Iliotibial band
Adductor magnus
Adductor longus
Gracilis

Execution

1. Start in an athletic position, with your feet shoulder-width apart, knees slightly bent, and eyes forward. Stand at the baseline center mark with the racket in your dominant hand.

2. Push off the right leg, and step the right foot over the left foot. Shuffle to the left by pushing off both feet and moving the left foot from behind the right foot and stepping to the left. Maintain a slight bend in the knees, and keep your shoulders back.

3. Repeat the movement to the right side of the baseline center mark, making sure that the first step after changing directions is a crossover step.

Muscles Involved

Primary: Adductor longus, adductor brevis, adductor magnus, gracilis, gluteus medius, iliotibial band

Secondary: Transversus abdominis, tensor fasciae latae, gluteus maximus, gluteus minimus

Tennis Focus

The lateral shuffle is the most common movement along the baseline during a rally. Often a crossover step is the first step made after a player changes directions along the baseline. It is important to replicate this movement in training with racket in hand. This movement most often occurs when a player has few time constraints and plays mostly neutral shots. The abductors and adductors along with the gluteus medius help maintain a low center of mass as you shuffle laterally to get in position to hit a well-balanced groundstroke. The speed at which players recover from wide balls typically separates the best players from the average. A faster crossover, or recovery, step allows you to get back into a successful position for your next stroke.

VARIATION

Weighted Lateral Shuffle With Crossover

You can perform the same movement pattern while holding a medicine ball in front of your body at hip height, or you can wear a weighted vest as you perform the movement. This increases the force required to perform the movement pattern.

Groundstroke Recovery

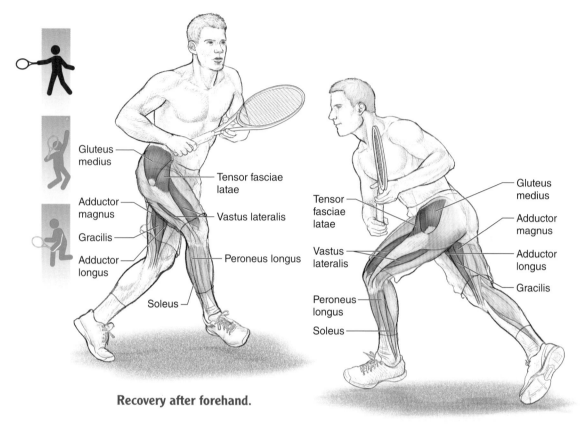

Gluteus
medius

Tensor fasciae
latae

Adductor
magnus

Vastus lateralis

Gracilis

Adductor
longus

Peroneus longus

Soleus

Recovery after forehand.

Tensor
fasciae
latae

Vastus
lateralis

Peroneus
longus

Soleus

Gluteus
medius

Adductor
magnus

Adductor
longus

Gracilis

Recovery after backhand.

Execution for Forehand

1. Start in an athletic position at the baseline center mark, racket in your dominant hand.
2. While maintaining a low, balanced center of mass, shuffle to the right for five shuffles, and perform a full forehand stroke.
3. Push off the outside right leg, and bring the right foot in front of your left leg to initiate the recovery movement to center court. Once the right leg lands on the left side of your body, continue to shuffle back to the starting position. Repeat the movement, maintaining good form as well as stroke technique.

Execution for Backhand

1. Perform the same movement to the other side, working on the backhand. Start in an athletic position at the baseline center mark, racket in your dominant hand.
2. While maintaining a low, balanced center of mass, shuffle to the left for five shuffles, and perform a full backhand stroke.

3. Push off the outside left leg, and bring the left foot in front of your right leg to initiate the recovery movement to center court. Once the left leg lands on the right side of your body, continue to shuffle back to the starting position. Repeat the movement, maintaining good form as well as stroke technique.

Muscles Involved

Primary: Vastus lateralis, iliacus, psoas major, gluteus medius, gluteus minimus, adductor longus, adductor brevis, adductor magnus, gracilis, tensor fasciae latae

Secondary: Soleus, peroneus longus

Tennis Focus

During the recovery step after a stroke, the best tennis players separate themselves from the rest in the movement department. The ability to hit a strong shot and then recover to an effective court position to execute the next stroke will give you a decided advantage. The muscles involved in this movement include the adductors, which help bring your leg in toward your body; the hip flexors; and the internal hip rotators. It is vital that you maintain a low center of mass and that the outside leg push against the ground is powerful.

VARIATION

Diagonal Recovery

The diagonal recovery variation of this exercise will help you fully develop tennis movement. The diagonal variations—moving diagonally forward and diagonally backward—simulate moving up for a short wide ball and back for a deep wide ball. For most movements, the quickest recovery step is the front crossover. However, for a short wide ball you may want to use a backward crossover step if your goal is to return to the center baseline.

Spider Drill

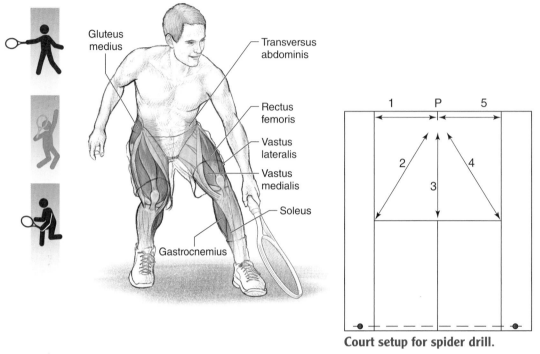

Court setup for spider drill.

Execution

1. Typically this drill is timed for speed. Start in an athletic position at the center mark on the baseline. You can perform this drill with or without a racket in your hand. Sprint from the center mark on the baseline to the corner of the baseline and right singles sideline. Touch the corner with your foot. Return and touch the center mark.

2. Sprint to the corner formed by the right singles sideline and the service line. Touch the corner with your foot. Return and touch the center mark.

3. Sprint to the T. Touch the T with your foot. Return and touch the center mark.

4. Sprint to the corner formed by the left singles sideline and the service line. Touch the corner with your foot. Return and touch the center mark.

5. Sprint to the corner formed by the baseline and the left singles sideline. Touch the corner with your foot. Return and touch the center mark.

Muscles Involved

Primary: Rectus femoris, vastus lateralis, vastus medialis, vastus intermedius, biceps femoris, semitendinosus, semimembranosus, gluteus maximus, gluteus medius, gastrocnemius, soleus

Secondary: Transversus abdominis, erector spinae, multifidus

Tennis Focus

Of all the drills that can be performed to improve movement skills, the spider drill might be the most tennis specific. It incorporates movement in all directions, and the distances covered are the same as those that would occur in an actual tennis match. The stopping and starting nature of the drill also mimics situations that happen in a tennis match. In this drill, players learn to maintain balance while sprinting from station to station. To make it even more tennis specific, perform the drill with racket in hand. You can also incorporate different movements such as moving laterally, shuffling, or back-pedaling.

VARIATION

Ball-Pickup Spider Drill

Perform the drill as described, only pick up a tennis ball at each station and return it to the center mark on the baseline. In addition, if you are not being timed during this drill, simulate hitting a shot when you arrive at each station. Hit forehands on the right side and backhands on the left side, or focus on one shot during each rotation.

Split Step

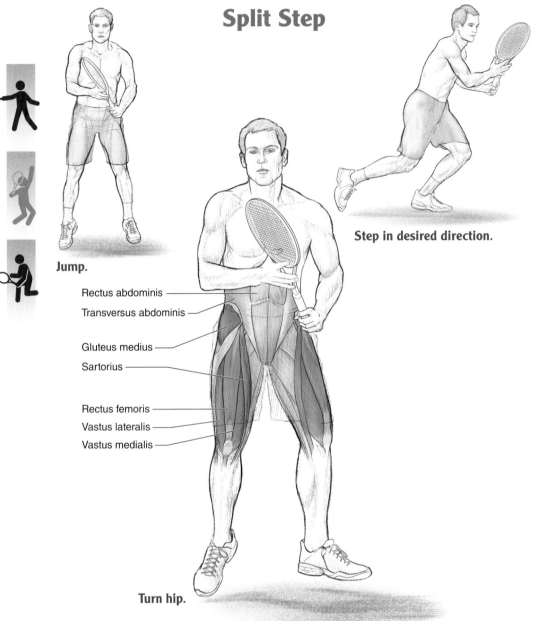

Jump.

Step in desired direction.

Rectus abdominis

Transversus abdominis

Gluteus medius

Sartorius

Rectus femoris

Vastus lateralis

Vastus medialis

Turn hip.

Execution

1. Start in an athletic position, with your feet shoulder-width apart, knees slightly bent, and eyes forward. Stand at the center mark on the baseline with a racket in your dominant hand.

2. Jump up but not too high. At the top of the jump and during the descent, turn your hip in the direction you intend to move. This is a simple unweighting-technique hop straight up and down, with the foot closest to the ball turning out slightly.

3. Once you land, take three or four steps in the direction of your intended final position. Repeat this movement pattern to the other side.

Muscles Involved

Primary: Rectus femoris, vastus lateralis, vastus medialis, vastus intermedius, biceps femoris, semitendinosus, semimembranosus, gluteus maximus, gluteus medius, sartorius

Secondary: Transversus abdominis, iliacus, psoas major, rectus abdominis

Tennis Focus

The split step is the most important movement skill in tennis. It is required before every tennis stroke except the serve. The timing of the split step is vital for putting you in great position for your next stroke. During the split step, the hip extensors contract concentrically to elevate you from the ground, the external hip rotators turn your hip and leg in the direction you want to move once you land, and the hip flexors work eccentrically during the landing to absorb the forces, reducing the shock to the joints.

Split Step With Stimulus

As a movement, the split step is not highly complex, but it becomes more complex when different stimuli are added. When you need to respond to an opponent's shot, the timing of the split step is crucial. Typically, the split step is initiated when the opponent starts the forward swing. To improve the timing of your split step, ask a coach or partner to either drop a ball for you to react to or feed you balls so you can hit shots during the drill.

Monster Walk

Transversus abdominis
Tensor fasciae latae
Gluteus medius
Gluteus maximus

Execution

1. Place a thin resistance band around your calves, and assume an athletic position with your feet shoulder-width apart, knees slightly bent, and eyes forward. Hold a racket in your dominant hand. Lower your starting position so that your thighs are parallel to the ground and your knees are bent approximately 90 degrees.

2. While maintaining an erect upper body and the approximately 90-degree knee angle, take a small step with your right leg to the right followed by a small step with your left leg to the right to return to your starting body position.

3. Repeat this movement to the right for 5 to 10 steps, and then perform the same movement to the left for 5 to 10 steps.

Muscles Involved

Primary: Gluteus medius, gluteus minimus, tensor fasciae latae

Secondary: Gluteus maximus, iliacus, psoas major, transversus abdominis, erector spinae

Tennis Focus

Because lateral movement is such an important component of tennis, developing strength and stability in the smaller muscles not only improves your ability to move well but also helps reduce the risk of injuries to the hips, thighs, and core. Also, many tennis strokes and movements are performed while the player is on one leg, which requires great single-leg stability to transfer power into the stroke or movement. The monster walk is one of the best exercises to improve single-leg stability, especially in the gluteus medius, one of the most important hip stabilizers. Most players who struggle to hit effective shots when stretched wide or deep are typically weak in the gluteus medius.

VARIATION

Diagonal Monster Walk

Perform the monster walk, but move in a diagonal rather than lateral direction. Step forward at an approximately 45-degree angle. The diagonal direction adds greater distance between steps, which activates muscles involved in the movements typically seen in semi-open groundstrokes and low volleys.

COMMON TENNIS INJURIES 10

Tennis players of all levels would like to improve their performance on the court. However, just as important is the prevention of injuries. In fact, training to enhance performance and to prevent injury often go hand in hand. Although typically relatively minor, injuries can and do occur in tennis. Injuries can be acute, such as an ankle sprain, or chronic, such as persistent shoulder pain. In either case, much can be done to prevent injuries by designing and following a proper conditioning program as well as playing with equipment appropriate for your game.

Selecting the Right Equipment

To select the right racket for your game, we recommend that you consult with a certified tennis instructor. A certified tennis instructor will help you choose the right type of racket based on length, weight, weight distribution, and material as well as determine the type and tension of the strings for your racket.

Rackets vary in stiffness, and stiffer rackets, although more powerful, could potentially cause excessive shock at impact. Lighter rackets are easier to manipulate but may absorb less impact stress. A heavy racket can be more difficult to maneuver, which could lead to late hits. A good coach or teaching professional can guide you to the right equipment. A certified tennis teaching professional also can recommend appropriate equipment for younger players or players who are not as strong to give them time to gradually get used to bigger and heavier rackets. An added benefit of consulting with a certified tennis teaching professional is that taking a few lessons will help you learn proper stroke technique, which also will cut down on the number of injuries.

Beyond selecting the appropriate racket for your game type, size, and strength, consider the type of surface you prefer to play on. Clay and grass courts typically tend to be a bit more forgiving on the body than hard court surfaces, but clay court surfaces can require greater strength and flexibility in the hips and legs because of the sliding required to get to shots. Shoe manufacturers make surface-specific shoes that are available at most sporting goods stores and tennis clubs. The key to selecting a good tennis shoe is to make sure the shoe provides sufficient lateral support in addition to cushioning. A knowledgeable person at a sporting goods store or a certified tennis teaching professional should be able to advise you regarding the appropriate shoe for your game, body type, and court surface.

Finally, since tennis is often played in warm environments, be sure to wear light-colored, loose-fitting clothing. A hat or visor will protect you from the sun. Wear sunscreen, and properly hydrate before, during, and after play to prevent many problems and heat-related illnesses.

Creating Body Balance

Tennis is played from the ground up. You create force by pushing against the ground and then transfer that force through your body into the racket. This system of force transfer is called a kinetic link or kinetic chain; each segment contributes sequentially to the total outcome of the stroke.

Since these forces are transferred from the ground up, muscles, joints, ligaments, and tendons from the ankles all the way through the wrist and fingers are influenced by how well or how poorly this transfer occurs. This clearly points out the need for balanced strength and flexibility of the lower and upper body. Equally important is the balance between the front and back of the body as well as the left and right sides. It may not be easy to develop this balance because tennis tends to be a somewhat one-sided sport in which the dominant side, particularly in the upper body, gets used more actively. In addition, generally the upper body muscles tend to work more concentrically in the front of the body and more eccentrically in the back during tennis strokes. A well-designed conditioning program can assist in overcoming many of these potential imbalances.

Research shows no significant differences in either strength or flexibility between the right and left sides of the lower body. This is an advantage when preventing and treating injuries in the lower body. Sometimes a tennis player's landing leg on the serve (the left leg for a right-handed server) is stronger because of the increased number of single-leg landings as a result of hitting serves.

In the upper body, typically strength and flexibility differences exist between the dominant and nondominant sides and the front and back of the body. Because of the nature of the sport, obtaining true balance between front and back or left and right is almost impossible, but this can be something to strive for in training and rehabilitation from injury. Since a major focus of a solid conditioning program should be striving for muscular balance, consider consulting with a certified expert in that field such as a strength and conditioning specialist to help prevent many types of injuries and allow you to reach your maximum performance potential.

Preventing Tennis Injuries

A review of the incidence of injury in tennis has found that injury rates are relatively low. For every 1,000 hours an athlete is on the court practicing or competing, he is likely to incur 2 to 20 injuries. This equates to .002 to .02 percent of playing time resulting in injury (W.B. Kibler and M. Safran, 2005, "Tennis Injuries," *Medicine and Sport Science*, 48: 120-137). Compared with other sports, this is a very low injury rate, but injuries still exist in tennis, and many of these injuries are a result of poor preparation and training.

Joint injuries are the most common tennis injuries. The key to preventing injuries to the joints is to make sure the surrounding muscle groups and associated ligaments and tendons are strong and flexible. Again this relates to the issue of balance. Of course acute injuries such as ankle sprains or bruises caused by collisions with fences or net posts can always occur, but proper training can help prevent many chronic injuries. Typically, chronic injuries in tennis fall in the category of overuse injuries.

Most tennis strokes are hit in a repetitive pattern, which can lead to overuse injuries (table 10.1, page 184). The most common types of overuse injuries in tennis occur to the shoulder from hitting thousands of serves and groundstrokes over time; the elbow, often related to improper technique or equipment; the lower back and abdominals from twisting and turning over an extended period of time and hitting with an open stance; and the knees and hips because of the stopping and starting nature of the sport. In addition, the lower legs and feet can take a beating from regular play on hard courts and the frequent changes of direction during a match. The most common injuries of the lower legs and feet include calf strains, shin splints, and plantar fasciitis. As you can see, tennis injuries can happen to all parts of the body. Following the exercises outlined in the previous chapters can help provide a balanced approach to training. The key is to strengthen the muscles surrounding each joint to help prevent many injuries. Figure 10.1 illustrates the most common injury sites in tennis players.

Upper body
26–31%

Body core
16–20%

Lower body
39–51%

a   *b*

Figure 10.1   Most common injury sites in tennis players: *(a)* front; *(b)* back.

Table 10.1 Common Overuse Injuries in Tennis

Part of the body	Injury	Symptoms	Causes	Prevention and treatment
Shoulders	Rotator cuff impingement	Pain during overhead motions or when lifting heavy weights	Muscle fatigue Improper technique, especially during overhead motions, that pinch the rotator cuff tendon	Use a proper strengthening and stretching program that includes the exercises in this chapter. Play with proper technique. Strengthen the shoulder and upper back muscles.
	Tendinitis	Pain in the posterior rotator cuff muscle and tendon area Pain in front of the shoulder that could be related to tendinitis in the biceps tendon	Overuse due to stress placed on the shoulder joint typically during the follow-through phase of the swing on groundstrokes and serves, resulting in repetitive microtrauma to the tendon	The exercises that prevent rotator cuff impingement also prevent tendinitis.
Elbows	Elbow epicondylitis	Pain on the outside of the elbow (lateral epicondylitis, or tennis elbow) Pain on the inside of the elbow (medial epicondylitis, or golfer's elbow). Medial epicondylitis involves the tendons that flex the wrist on forehands and serves and occurs more often in skilled players.	Improper backhand technique Hitting the ball late on a backhand	Take tennis lessons to make sure you have proper stroke technique. Strengthen the flexors and extensors of the forearms using light weights. Stretch the flexors and extensors of the forearms.
Wrists	Wrist pain	Pain on the radial or ulnar side of the wrist Pain during radial deviation is less common in tennis players and typically involves the tendon on the radial (thumb) side.	Pain on the ulnar side may be due to ulnar deviation prior to acceleration of the two-handed backhand. Improper technique Stiff racket Extreme grip Powerful strokes	The exercises that prevent elbow injuries also prevent wrist injuries.

Part of the body	Injury	Symptoms	Causes	Prevention and treatment
Lower back	Lower back strain	Pain in the lower back due to acute injury from a sudden, unexpected move or overuse from a long match or series of long matches with a lot of stopping and starting	Inadequate trunk strength to handle the high demand for trunk rotation, especially during open-stance groundstrokes	Proper stretching and strengthening of the lower back muscles, hamstrings, and deep hip rotators
Abdominals	Abdominal strain or abdominal muscle pull	Pain in the core, especially when hitting high balls or stretching for wide shots	Increased demand for trunk rotation during open-stance groundstrokes High-speed serves	Exercises that strengthen the abdominal muscles, lower back muscles, and obliques
Knees	Knee pain	Irritation or pain behind the knee cap or near the patella	Lack of strength or support from the muscles surrounding the knee. Without this muscular support, the knee cap will not glide properly in the groove at the end of the femur.	Knee braces can help support the knee, but strengthening the quadriceps muscles and increasing their range of motion is most beneficial. Avoid exercises that require more than 90 degrees of flexion, such as deep knee squats.
Hips	Hip flexor strain	Difficulty moving on the court Pain or discomfort in the hip	Open-stance groundstrokes Frequent changes of direction Tightness in the hamstrings and quadriceps	Develop good flexibility in the hips. Strengthen and stretch the hamstrings, quadriceps, and lower back. Stretch daily.
Lower legs	Calf muscle strain, or tennis leg	Pain on the medial side of the gastrocnemius that feels as if someone has just hit you with a ball	Overuse Frequent landing on the forefoot	Stretch and strengthen the gastrocnemius and soleus. After an injury of this type, do not rush back to play too soon. This injury tends to recur if not allowed to properly heal.

(continued)

Table 10.1   *(continued)*

Part of the body	Injury	Symptoms	Causes	Prevention and treatment
Lower legs *(continued)*	Shin splints	Pain in the front of the shin along the tibia	Chronic inflammation of the fibrous tissue that covers the muscle or bone of the lower leg Switching court surfaces Significant pronation Often seen in young players who are going through growth spurts	Rest. Avoid pain-causing activities. Stretch and strengthen the muscle. Orthotics may help rehabilitation and may prevent the condition from recurring.
Feet	Plantar fasciitis	Pain at the bottom of the foot just in front of the heel, usually greatest when weight is put on the foot and when you first get up in the morning; extension of the toes and toe raises typically cause the greatest pain.	Not clear but likely has to do with the loading phase of the strokes; during plantar flexion, the toes are forced into hyperextension, which puts a maximum stretch on the plantar fascia.	Stretch and wear orthotics to rehabilitate. Rest immediately after being injured or feeling pain. Wear heel cups to cushion the heel during touch-down.

In the remainder of this chapter, we outline some of the most relevant exercises and stretches to prevent common tennis injuries. Perform the strength exercises related to injury prevention every other day to give your body a rest in between. Flexibility exercises should be performed daily as your schedule permits. Because flexibility exercises are most beneficial when the muscles are warm, consider working on flexibility after an on-court training session or match.

Calf Stretch

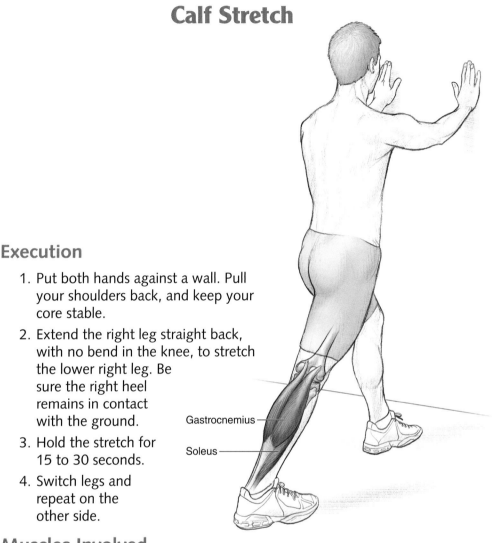

Execution

1. Put both hands against a wall. Pull your shoulders back, and keep your core stable.

2. Extend the right leg straight back, with no bend in the knee, to stretch the lower right leg. Be sure the right heel remains in contact with the ground.

3. Hold the stretch for 15 to 30 seconds.

4. Switch legs and repeat on the other side.

Gastrocnemius

Soleus

Muscles Involved

Primary: Gastrocnemius, soleus

Secondary: Popliteus

Tennis Focus

Many tennis players experience pain or discomfort in the calf. In many instances, lack of appropriate range of motion contributes to lower leg injuries. Lack of appropriate range of motion can also limit performance on the court since the two major muscles of the lower leg—the gastrocnemius and soleus—are the first stop in the kinetic chain from the ground up to the ultimate goal of sending power into the ball. Calf pain or a tight feeling in the calf usually is experienced more often if a player plays the majority of time on a hard court. It also is common for players to complain of calf pain when they transition from playing on clay or grass courts to playing on hard courts.

Standing Balance on Wobble Board

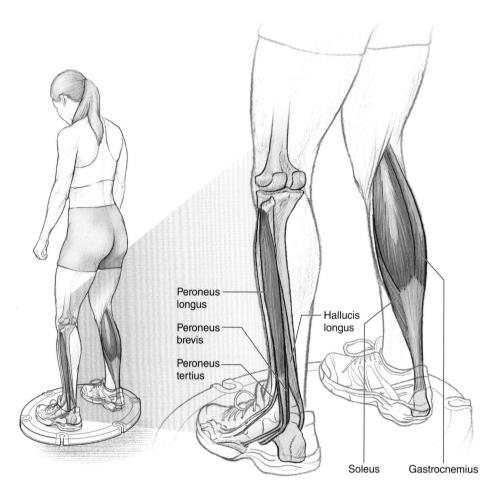

Peroneus longus

Peroneus brevis

Peroneus tertius

Hallucis longus

Soleus

Gastrocnemius

Execution

1. Slowly stand on a wobble board. Keep your feet shoulder-width apart, your core contracted, and your shoulder blades back.

2. Attempt to maintain your balance with no movement.

3. Hold the position for 30 to 60 seconds.

Muscles Involved

Primary: Peroneus longus, peroneus brevis, gastrocnemius, soleus

Secondary: Hallucis longus, anterior tibialis, peroneus tertius

Tennis Focus

This exercise helps develop proprioception, or body awareness, in the lower body and can directly improve a tennis player's balance. Balance is important on the court because most strokes and movements are played in traditionally unstable environments, such as a single-leg position. The more body awareness an athlete has, the better she can transfer her weight into the strokes, resulting in greater ball velocities. This greater body awareness also is beneficial in potentially limiting the likelihood of injuries, especially in the lower body.

VARIATION

Standing Balance on Other Uneven Surfaces

Variations of this exercise take many forms. You can perform the same exercise on one leg, while holding a medicine ball or dumbbell, or even while blindfolded. All these variations increase the difficulty of the exercise and are good progressive exercises to improve proprioception and balance for the tennis player.

Side Ankle Walk

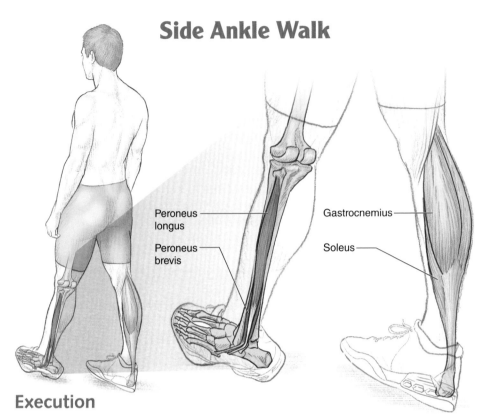

Peroneus longus

Peroneus brevis

Gastrocnemius

Soleus

Execution

1. Stand with feet shoulder-width apart. Shift your weight so you are balancing on the sides of your feet.
2. Take a step forward on the side of your left foot followed by a step on the side of your right foot.
3. Repeat, alternating steps, until you have taken five steps on each foot.

Muscles Involved

Primary: Peroneus longus, peroneus brevis

Secondary: Gastrocnemius, soleus

Tennis Focus

Ankle injuries occur in tennis because of the rapid changes of direction and the large forces that the ankle joints endure during play. The side ankle walk is a great way to strengthen the muscles, ligaments, and tendons in the ankles. Strengthening these ankle structures may help prevent an inversion ankle sprain, the most typical ankle injury experienced during tennis play. An inversion ankle sprain occurs when the ankle rolls over on the outside, or lateral aspect, of the foot. The most typical damage experienced is to the talofibular ligament; in more severe sprains, the calcaneofibular ligament can also be damaged. Ankle sprains are acute injuries that typically occur when the player is running for a wide ball or when the player makes a quick, abrasive change of direction. A routine that includes side ankle walks can help strengthen the ankles, which should help offset the occurrence of ankle injuries.

Heel Walk

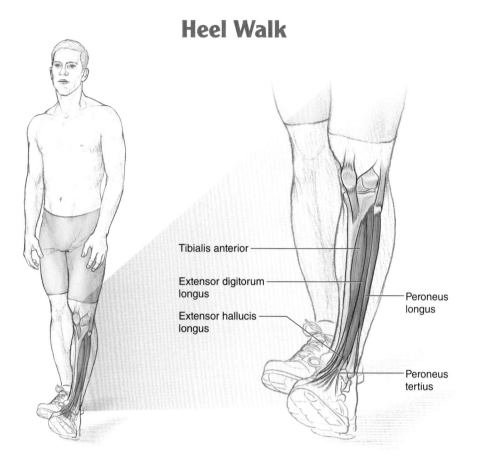

Tibialis anterior

Extensor digitorum longus

Extensor hallucis longus

Peroneus longus

Peroneus tertius

Execution

1. Stand with feet shoulder-width apart.
2. Step forward on the heel of your left foot, toes off the ground and pointing to the sky. Step forward on the heel of your right foot, toes off the ground and pointing to the sky.
3. Repeat, alternating feet, until you have taken five steps with each foot.

Muscles Involved

Primary: Tibialis anterior, extensor digitorum longus, extensor hallucis longus, peroneus longus, peroneus tertius

Tennis Focus

The heel walk develops strength in the muscles, ligaments, and tendons around the ankle. However, the greatest benefit of the heel walk is that it strengthens the anterior tibialis muscle, which helps limit the occurrences of shin splints and shin-related pain. This is a vitally important exercise, especially for tennis players who have limited ankle strength and experience shin-related pain.

Kneeling Hip Flexor Stretch

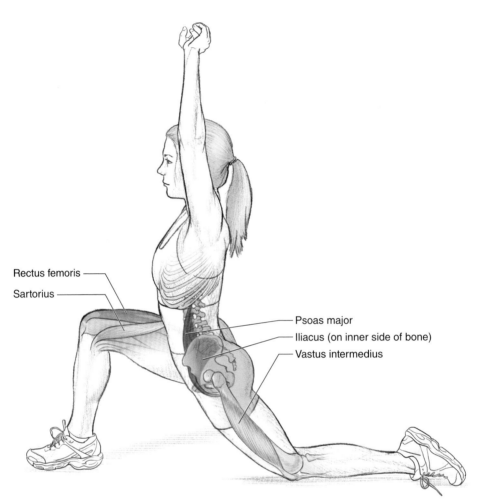

Rectus femoris
Sartorius

Psoas major
Iliacus (on inner side of bone)
Vastus intermedius

Execution

1. Kneel with your left knee on the floor (or on a cushion, towel, or mat to reduce the strain on the knee). Step the right foot forward, and lunge so the right knee is flexed at 90 degrees. Extend your arms overhead, with elbows straight and hands touching.

2. Slowly push the left hip forward to increase the stretch in the left hip flexor. Make sure your right knee does not extend over your right foot.

3. Hold the stretch for 15 to 30 seconds.

4. Repeat the stretch on the opposite leg.

Muscles Involved

Primary: Iliacus, psoas major, rectus femoris

Secondary: Vastus intermedius, sartorius

Tennis Focus

A tennis player's hip flexor muscles are continually under stress. Great tennis movement requires the player to be in a low athletic position while moving as well as during most strokes. Although this low position is ideal for quicker movements and greater weight transfer during groundstrokes and volleys (which is a great thing!), it also shortens the muscles of the hip flexors (which is a bad thing). This can lead to injury and reduced range of motion, which can limit performance. The kneeling hip flexor stretch can help increase or at least maintain the length of the hip flexors, which can improve movement on the court as well as help reduce hip- and core-related injuries.

Tennis Ball Massage

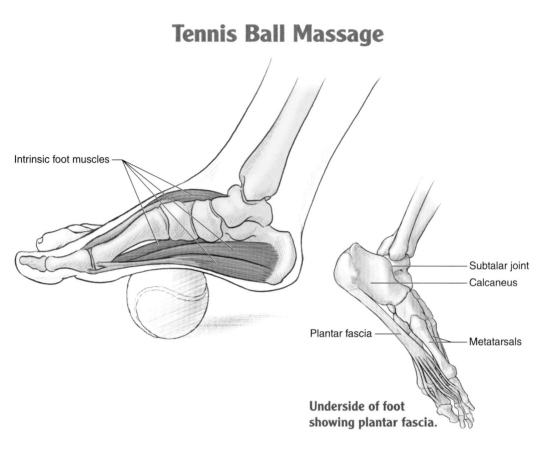

Intrinsic foot muscles

Subtalar joint

Calcaneus

Plantar fascia

Metatarsals

Underside of foot showing plantar fascia.

Execution

1. Sit on a bench or chair. Place your bare foot on a tennis ball. The tennis ball is underneath the middle of your foot.

2. Slowly move your foot forward, backward, and in a circular manner to massage the bottom of your foot for 30 seconds or until your pain or tightness releases.

3. Switch feet and repeat the process with the other foot.

Muscles Involved

Primary: Intrinsic foot muscles

Tennis Focus

The tennis ball massage is not so much an exercise as it is a recovery technique. It will keep the bottom of your foot loose and reduce tightness that can be caused by excessive ground contact and changes of direction often required during tennis practice and competition. It also is a good technique to reduce heel and midfoot tightness and can relieve the pain caused by plantar fasciitis. The plantar fascia is a thick, fibrous band of connective tissue that originates on the bottom surface of the calcaneus (heel bone) and extends along the sole of the foot toward the toes.

Lying Knee to Chest Stretch

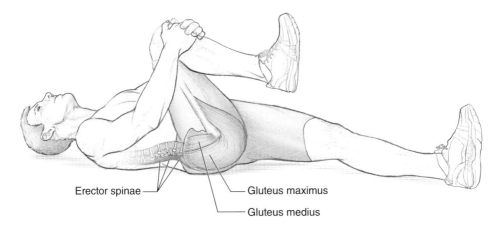

Erector spinae ——————   —— Gluteus maximus
——— Gluteus medius

Execution

1. Lie supine on the floor or a mat. Relax your shoulders. Fully extend your legs and feet, pointing your toes to the sky.
2. With both hands, grasp your right leg just below the knee. Pull your right leg toward your chest by flexing your knee.
3. Hold the stretch for 15 to 30 seconds.
4. Return to the starting position and switch legs. Repeat the stretch on the opposite leg.

Muscles Involved

Primary: Erector spinae, multifidus

Secondary: Gluteus maximus, gluteus medius

Tennis Focus

In tennis players, the lower back is one of the most injured areas in the entire body. Although many things can lead to injury, one predisposing factor is lack of flexibility in the lower back. The lying knee to chest stretch is a great exercise to improve lower back flexibility. A structured strengthening program for the lower back can greatly reduce the chance of lower back injuries in the future. The exercises in chapters 5 and 6 also will strengthen the back and core muscles.

Lying Hamstring Stretch

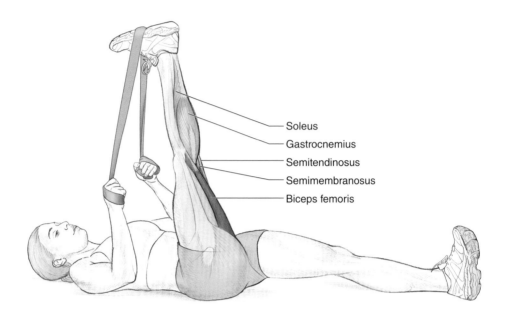

Soleus
Gastrocnemius
Semitendinosus
Semimembranosus
Biceps femoris

Execution

1. Lie supine with shoulders on the floor and legs straight out, toes pointed to the sky. Place a resistance band, a rope, or a towel around your right foot.
2. Pull on the ends of the resistance band to lift the right leg straight up.
3. Hold the stretch at the highest point for 15 to 30 seconds.
4. Return to the starting position and switch legs. Repeat the stretch on the opposite leg.

Muscles Involved

Primary: Biceps femoris, semitendinosus, semimembranosus

Secondary: Popliteus, gastrocnemius, soleus

Tennis Focus

The hamstrings (the biceps femoris, semitendinosus, and semimembranosus) play a major role in hip extension during on-court movement and are heavily involved in deceleration movements during changes of direction. The hamstring group is one of the traditionally tight areas in tennis players. There is a relationship between hamstring tightness and lower back pain. Improving hamstring flexibility will reduce the chance of injury to the lower back and also will improve on-court movement.

Figure-Four Stretch

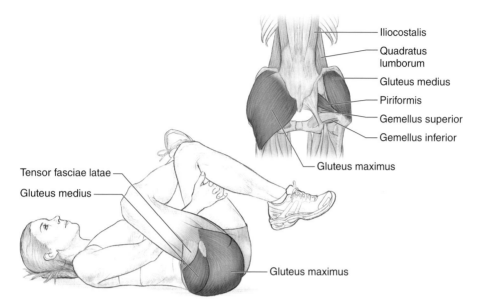

Iliocostalis

Quadratus lumborum

Gluteus medius

Piriformis

Gemellus superior

Gemellus inferior

Gluteus maximus

Tensor fasciae latae

Gluteus medius

Gluteus maximus

Execution

1. Lie supine on the floor. Put your right malleolus bone (the bone on the outside of the ankle) on your left quadriceps, just above the left knee.
2. Put your right hand between your legs and your left hand around your left leg.
3. With both hands, pull back on the left leg to increase the stretch in the hamstrings.
4. Hold for 15 to 30 seconds.
5. Return to the starting position and switch legs. Repeat the stretch on the opposite leg.

Muscles Involved

Primary: Gluteus maximus, piriformis, gluteus medius

Secondary: Iliocostalis, quadratus lumborum, gemellus superior, gemellus inferior, tensor fasciae latae, sartorius

Tennis Focus

The major muscles in an athlete's posterior region are under a lot of stress during tennis play because of the requirement to transfer weight in tennis strokes and the maintenance of a low center of mass during movement. These muscles are required to be in a shortened, tensed position throughout tennis practice and match play. Therefore, it is important to maintain an optimal length in these muscles, which will allow for full rotation at the hips and an effective transfer of weight from the ground up through the kinetic chain and ultimately an effective energy transfer into the ball.

Forearm Extensor Stretch

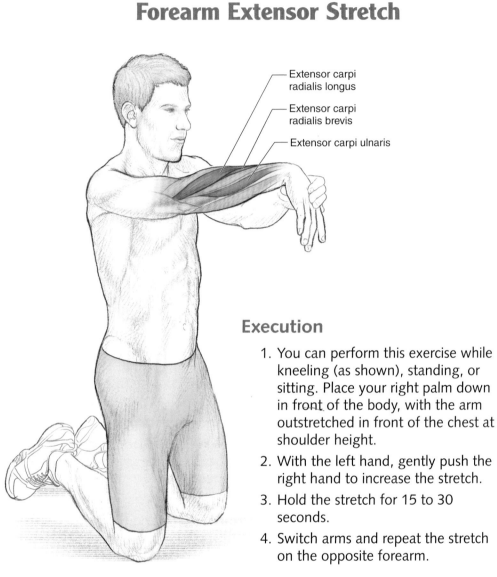

Extensor carpi radialis longus

Extensor carpi radialis brevis

Extensor carpi ulnaris

Execution

1. You can perform this exercise while kneeling (as shown), standing, or sitting. Place your right palm down in front of the body, with the arm outstretched in front of the chest at shoulder height.

2. With the left hand, gently push the right hand to increase the stretch.

3. Hold the stretch for 15 to 30 seconds.

4. Switch arms and repeat the stretch on the opposite forearm.

Muscles Involved

Primary: Extensor carpi ulnaris, extensor carpi radialis longus, extensor carpi radialis brevis

Tennis Focus

Flexibility in the forearm extensors is vitally important for most tennis strokes, but it directly influences the quality of the backswing on the backhand groundstroke. The greater the functional range of motion, the greater the capability to store potential energy that can be released during the acceleration stage of the groundstroke.

Forearm Flexor Stretch

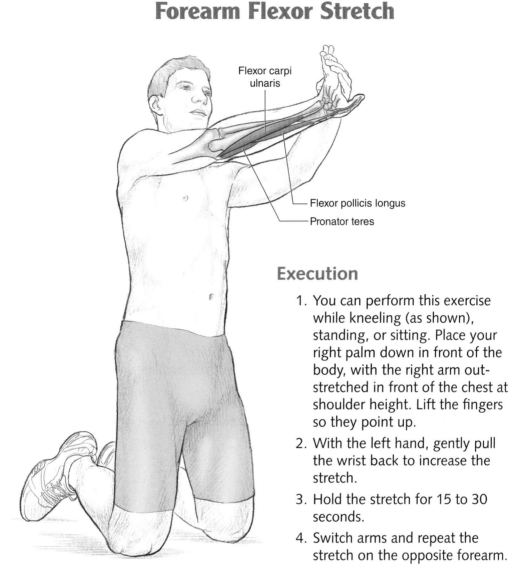

Flexor carpi ulnaris

Flexor pollicis longus

Pronator teres

Execution

1. You can perform this exercise while kneeling (as shown), standing, or sitting. Place your right palm down in front of the body, with the right arm outstretched in front of the chest at shoulder height. Lift the fingers so they point up.
2. With the left hand, gently pull the wrist back to increase the stretch.
3. Hold the stretch for 15 to 30 seconds.
4. Switch arms and repeat the stretch on the opposite forearm.

Muscles Involved

Primary: Flexor carpi ulnaris, flexor pollicis longus, pronator teres

Tennis Focus

The importance of appropriate flexibility in the forearm flexors cannot be underestimated. Appropriate flexibility in the forearms is vital for efficient stroke mechanics because this area is one of the last segments of the body to transfer energy to the ball at contact. An athlete with poor flexibility will experience limited stroke mechanics caused by limited range of motion, thereby reducing power production and on-court performance. Also, poor range of motion can predispose an athlete to a greater likelihood of upper arm and shoulder problems, which could lead to injuries.

External Rotation With Shoulder Retraction

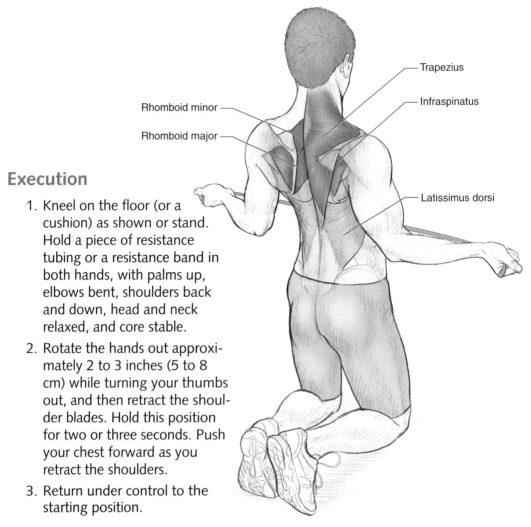

Rhomboid minor

Rhomboid major

Trapezius

Infraspinatus

Latissimus dorsi

Execution

1. Kneel on the floor (or a cushion) as shown or stand. Hold a piece of resistance tubing or a resistance band in both hands, with palms up, elbows bent, shoulders back and down, head and neck relaxed, and core stable.

2. Rotate the hands out approximately 2 to 3 inches (5 to 8 cm) while turning your thumbs out, and then retract the shoulder blades. Hold this position for two or three seconds. Push your chest forward as you retract the shoulders.

3. Return under control to the starting position.

Muscles Involved

Primary: Trapezius, infraspinatus, rhomboid major, rhomboid minor

Secondary: Latissimus dorsi

Tennis Focus

Because many overuse injuries occur at the shoulder joint, it is important to strengthen the rotator cuff as well as the scapular stabilizers. These muscles often work eccentrically, in particular during the follow-through phase of serves and forehands. This exercise will improve the integrity of the shoulder girdle by working the muscles in the opposite direction of their tennis function, which is concentric. Additionally, this particular exercise will help with proper posture, which is also a concern for many tennis players because of the repetitive nature of the sport.

EXERCISE FINDER

Core and Torso

Legs

Rotational Strengthening

Movement Drills

Common Tennis Injuries

ABOUT THE AUTHORS

E. Paul Roetert, PhD, is the Chief Executive Officer of the American Alliance for Health, Physical Education, Recreation, and Dance (AAHPERD), where he is responsible for promoting leadership, research, education, and best practices in the professions that support creative, healthy, and active lifestyles.

Prior to this position, Roetert was the Managing Director of the United State Tennis Association's (USTA's) Player Development Program and Tournament Director of the U.S. Open Junior Tennis Championships from 2002 to 2009. He has also served as the Executive Director of the American Sport Education Program (ASEP) and as the Administrator of Sport Science for the USTA, where he developed the sport science program.

Roetert has published extensively in the field of tennis, including several books, more than 20 book chapters, and over 100 articles. He is a Fellow in the American College of Sports Medicine, a Master Professional with the United States Professional Tennis Association (USPTA), and an Honorary Professional of the Professional Tennis Registry (PTR). He was the 2002 Educational Merit Award recipient from the International Tennis Hall of Fame for outstanding service to the game of tennis. Roetert holds a PhD in biomechanics from the University of Connecticut.

Mark S. Kovacs, PhD, is the Senior Manager of Sport Science and Coaching Education for the United States Tennis Association (USTA). He was a collegiate All-American and NCAA doubles champion at Auburn University. After playing professionally, he pursued his graduate work performing tennis-specific research and has a graduate degree in exercise science and a PhD in exercise physiology.

Mark has published and presented tennis-specific research in numerous top scientific journals and at national and international conferences. He is an author of the tennis conditioning text *Tennis Training: Enhancing On-Court Performance* and is currently the Assistant Editor-in-Chief of the *Strength and Conditioning Journal*. Mark is also still actively working as a strength and conditioning specialist training elite professional tennis players, including athletes who have participated in all of the Grand Slam tournaments.

ANATOMY SERIES

Each book in the *Anatomy Series* provides detailed, full-color anatomical illustrations of the muscles in action and step-by-step instructions that detail perfect technique and form for each pose, exercise, movement, stretch, and stroke.

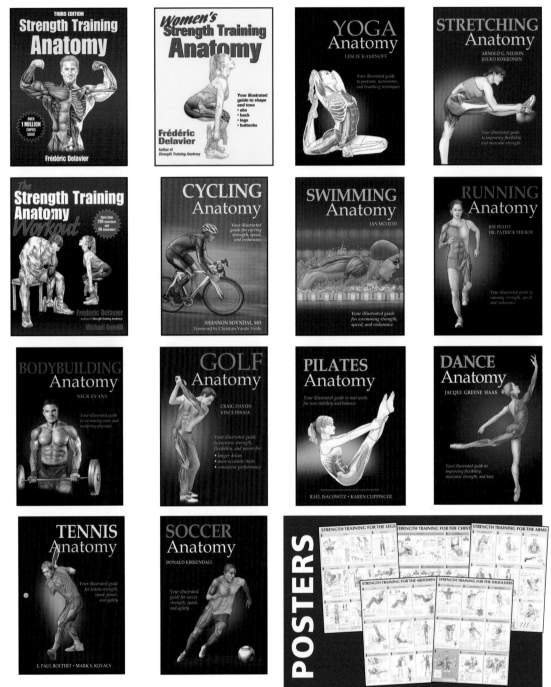

To place your order, U.S. customers call TOLL FREE **1-800-747-4457**
In Canada call 1-800-465-7301 • In Europe call +44 (0) 113 255 5665 • In Australia call 08 8372 0999
In New Zealand call 0800 222 062 • or visit **www.HumanKinetics.com/Anatomy**

HUMAN KINETICS
The Premier Publisher for Sports & Fitness
P.O. Box 5076, Champaign, IL 61825-5076